A New You

PEARSON
Prentice Hall
LIFE

Prentice Hall LIFE

If life is what you make it, then making it better starts here.

What we learn today can change our lives tomorrow. It can change our goals or change our minds; open up new opportunities or simply inspire us to make a difference. That's why we have created a new breed of books that do more to help you make more of *your* life.

Whether you want more confidence or less stress, a new skill or a different perspective, we've designed *Prentice Hall Life* books to help you to make a change for the better. Together with our authors we share a commitment to bring you the brightest ideas and best ways to manage your life, work and wealth.

In these pages we hope you'll find the ideas you need for the life *you* want. Go on, help yourself.

It's what you make it

* * *

A New You

The small changes that make the biggest difference to your life

Nicola Cook

PEARSON

Prentice Hall

LIFE

Harlow, England • London • New York • Boston • San Francisco • Toronto • Sydney • Singapore • Hong Kong
Tokyo • Seoul • Taipei • New Delhi • Cape Town • Madrid • Mexico City • Amsterdam • Munich • Paris • Milan

PEARSON EDUCATION LIMITED

Edinburgh Gate
Harlow CM20 2JE
Tel: +44 (0)1279 623623
Fax: +44 (0)1279 431059
Website: www.pearsoned.co.uk

First published in Great Britain in 2009

ISBN: 978-0-273-72269-4

British Library Cataloguing-in-Publication Data
A catalogue record for this book is available from the British Library

Library of Congress Cataloging-in-Publication Data
Cook, Nicola.
  A new you : the small changes that make the biggest difference to your life / Nicola Cook.
    p. cm.
  ISBN 978-0-273-72269-4 (pbk.)
  1. Change (Psychology) 2. Success–Psychological aspects. I. Title.
  BF637.C4C66 2008
  158.1–dc22
                          2008041915

10 9 8 7 6 5 4 3 2
12 11 10 09

Typeset in 10pt IowanOldStyle by 3
Printed and bound in Great Britain by Ashford Colour Press Ltd, Gosport, Hants

The Publisher's policy is to use paper manufactured from sustainable forests.

In memory of Siddle C. Cook

For being the most inspirational role model and the best Granddad a girl could have ever had.

Contents

Introduction

Are you ready for a change?

Is something not working in your life? Maybe there's something you want to do or be? Or perhaps you are simply wondering if there's more to life, and if so, how do you find that 'more'? Then you're in the right place. It's time to discover the power of possibility and reveal your full potential.

Whatever areas of your life need attention, this book is for you. Whether you feel underappreciated at work or 'stuck 'in a job you don't like. Whether a relationship has lost its fizz, or you can't seem to find that perfect partner. Whether your body isn't the way you'd like it to be or you feel held back by a lack of confidence. Or whether your life simply isn't what you'd hoped for.

Many of us have experienced times in life when we wish we could wave a magic wand and sort everything out, make everything better. Start again even – live a different life. Turn back time and do things differently. We wonder what it would be like if we were somebody else (usually somebody better looking, richer, more successful, more confident, happier and so on!).

Whatever your situation or however you're feeling, the answer isn't to be somebody else. Because, as it happens, there are things about you that are special, gifted and unique. Yes, even if you can't see it yourself some of the time (or any of the time). Trust me on this.

So what if we could keep all the special, unique and great bits about you, but lose the unhelpful bits, change whatever needs to change, get rid of the mental blocks that are holding you back and help you become all you could be? If that sounds good, then the great news is that it's entirely possible – and this book will show you how.

Creating solid foundations

Success in all areas of life is 80 per cent about having the right psychology and 20 per cent about having the right skills and know-how. There is absolutely no point in discovering new ways to make your life better unless you've got the desire to *want* to change your circumstances and have the right mindset in place. That's why this book is split into two parts.

The first part is designed to help you develop the right mindset for your success. You will identify your starting point, who you are (no, who you *really* are) and discover how you can change your psychology, creating the right stage on which you can live your life to the fullest, creating the success you really want.

The second part of the book will equip you with multiple skills and strategies to give you the practical know-how to make the difference in whichever area of your life you want to change.

Thinking big, doing small

There's a common pattern among those who have tried to change their lives but who have not managed to make it happen. It goes something like this:

- become dissatisfied with an area of life, and decide to do something about it
- attack that area of life with a radical plan to make change happen
- expect immediate massive results but discover this doesn't happen

■ feel discouraged, become disheartened and so give up until the next time the feeling of dissatisfaction resurfaces ... and so the destructive cycle continues.

There's a reason for this pattern. A rocket taking off into space uses up a huge amount of fuel, thrust and energy in order to take off. It gets the rocket out of the earth's atmosphere, but the incredible level of power isn't sustainable and eventually that fuel is spent and the rocket orbits earth aimlessly or returns empty. This is exactly what happens when you throw everything you have into massive action but don't see immediate results and can't keep it up.

It's the same pattern as the millions of people every year who start a very strict diet only to give up after a couple of weeks because they're hungry and miserable and find it too difficult to stick to. You may be full of good intentions but if the changes needed to achieve your goals in the short term appear too radical, you'll probably lose momentum and return to earth with a big crash!

However, there is another way. A more sustainable way. It's possible to achieve anything, simply by making smaller shifts in your behaviour, and committing to them over the long term.

For example, if you are massively in debt right now and feel you have a huge mountain to climb to turn your situation around, you have choices to make. You could hang your hopes on winning the Lottery every Saturday night, only to be disappointed when your numbers don't come up, or you could change your financial habits a little bit on a day-to-day basis. The small-steps route may take longer to turn your situation around than if you were to receive an unexpected windfall, but I guarantee that by taking consistent, constructive action you will achieve your goals, and you know you are doing something positive, rather than feeling desperate and hopeless.

If you're feeling overwhelmed because your current situation is a very long way away from where you want to be, it doesn't matter. The small-changes, long-term approach will get you there.

This is true for any situation in your life right now, whether you need to lose a lot of weight a kilo at a time, rebuild a relationship one day at a time, or find your professional niche and embark on a change in career one step at a time.

You simply need to stay focused on your long-term goals while committing to smaller sustainable changes in your behaviour on a day-to-day basis. The results that follow will last forever.

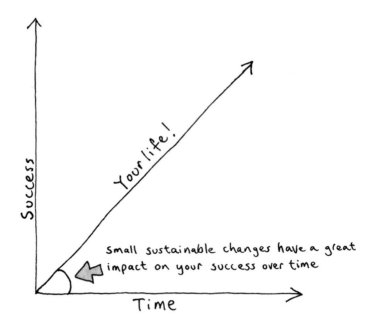

The small-change, long-term approach is the most effective way to make change and make it stick. Your underlying 'right mindset' is what will keep you focused on taking the right action over the long term – that's why we pay so much attention to it in this book. With the right mindset, everything flows so much more easily.

There's no need to take drastic action. No need to have to put yourself through the worry and angst of gearing up to do something huge. Instead, make a commitment to those smaller shifts and before very long the change will become obvious as everyone, including you, begins to notice the New You emerging.

No matter what is causing your frustration, no matter how lost you may be feeling, no matter how exhausted you may be, apply the philosophies and techniques in this book and you'll be able to make those small changes that really will have a huge impact on your life. Very soon you will notice the difference.

Part 1

Developing the right mindset

01

Stick a pin in it –
the power of new beginnings

Congratulations! Your journey to the New You has already begun. By deciding to read this book you have already made a huge commitment to a better life for you and all those who are close to you.

Every one of us has the opportunity to have a highly successful and fulfilling life in all areas. It is absolutely possible to find your passion and purpose, and base your working life around this, be financially secure, have a highly rewarding relationship, raise happy healthy children, find time for the things you really want to do, and fuel your life with the energy to live it to the maximum.

So where do you start? Before you embark on any journey, be it a road trip or a journey of personal change, it's vitally important to decide on your destination, set your course, find the right route map and then of course start moving in your chosen direction. Before any of that, however, there's something even more important to establish – your current position.

After all, how can you plan your route unless you know where you're starting from? If you want to go to London and have a roadmap of the UK, the map is completely useless unless you know where you are now – especially if it turns out your starting point is Las Vegas! In that case, your roadmap of the UK would be of no help whatsoever. To reach your destination you would now need a very different plan, strategy and use of resources.

HOW CAN YOU PLAN YOUR ROUTE UNLESS YOU KNOW WHERE YOU'RE STARTING FROM?

Do you know where you're starting from?

There was a reason you ended up reading this book. Maybe you know what the reason is, and you made the decision to read the book consciously, hoping it would help with something particular that's going on in your life. Perhaps you have no idea whatsoever: you simply bought it on impulse and just felt like taking it home. If that's the case, then great. I know that as you start to read further and then apply the techniques you will acquire insights and your reason will become clear.

Maybe you read a lot of books and are simply hoping to learn something interesting. If so, that's great too, and in this case don't worry about finding a problem to analyse where one doesn't exist. However, if you are aiming to make changes in some areas of your life then make sure you complete the exercises and take time to answer all of the questions.

Even if you think you know where you're starting from, it's worth making sure by following the questions below. In my 18 years experience of working with people, very often the issues we think we're dealing with are actually smoke and mirrors and we use these to cover up truer, deeper reasons for needing to make changes in our lives.

It's time to uncover what's really going on in your life right now. Do make a note of your answers to the questions below somewhere, as you will need to refer back to them later.

Questions always lead to answers

Very often all the information we need is right in front of us. We're simply not asking the right questions. Questions *always* lead to answers, as your brain *always* seeks the information. They are one of the most powerful tools you have available to you right now, both as you take the steps to reach the New You, but also in so many areas of your life. Asking the right questions can close a £1 million deal, reveal what's behind the behaviour of an upset child, or help you understand your past decisions, your choices and your current life. We will look at questions and how to use them throughout the book; here we are going to ask some tough questions to help you uncover the issues that are most concerning you right now.

Before you read on, take a moment to reflect on what things about yourself, and your life, you'd like to improve. What are you currently spending most of your time thinking and talking about? And are these thoughts primarily positive or negative?

You could be thinking of something very broad such 'my work', 'my relationship with x', 'my health' or 'my finances'. Or it could be very specific such as 'I need a purpose in life', 'I lack confidence in social situations', 'My partner never puts their dirty clothes in the laundry basket', 'I want to start a business, but don't know how to go about it' or 'I want to train for a new career but don't know how I can find the time or the money with my current commitments'. They may seem trivial, but if they are the things that are causing you to be stressed then they are important.

Now you have a few things in mind, take a moment to read the more specific questions below and jot down your answers.

Question:

What area or areas of your life are currently causing you the most stress? If you have identified more than one area, then complete the rest of the questions for each one.

Question:

How long has this area of your life been out of balance? Is it a recent problem or has it been festering for some time?

Question:

Is the problem being created by you, or by circumstances outside your control, perhaps by someone or something else?

For example, if your relationship has ended, was it your decision or was it your partner's choice (and you felt there was nothing you could do to change their mind)? Is your boss blocking your efforts to take on a more challenging role? Or do you run your own business, which is not making enough money and you can't seem to increase sales?

Question:

What do you feel when you think about the problem area or areas of your life?

Reflecting on this, some of your feelings may be positive but others may be draining and negative. From the two lists in the box on the next page, take a moment to reflect back on your recent past and select your top 10 feelings, based on how intensely you experience them, together with how frequently. Mark them in order, with 1 being the most intense and most frequent and 10 being the least intense and frequent. If none of these terms quite fit, add your own different, descriptive words if you like.

Note: you may not feel like this every moment of every day, but focus on what you generally feel when you think about the areas of your life that are causing you the most stress.

Question:

What do you say to yourself about this area of your life? If you had to use a phrase to describe how you feel, what would that be?

Question:

What is your intuition telling you that you need to act on?

Positive and negative feelings

Grateful	Fearful of change
Hopeful	Sad
Excited	Out of control
Happy	Weak
Joyful	Lost
Fulfilled	Unloved
Loved	Angry
Appreciated	Worried
Worthy	Lacking self-belief
Peaceful	Frightened
Certain	Doubtful
Focused	Indecisive
Sense of belonging	Insecure
Alive	Depressed
Fun-filled	Not good enough
Energetic	Worn out
Healthy	Fearful of the unknown
Secure	Overwhelmed
Embracing life	Guilty

Question:

Why have you not taken action before now? What has been stopping you?

Reflecting on your answers

As you reflect on your answers, I would hazard a guess that it has become blatantly obvious which is the area or areas of your life you need to work on (and this may not have been the initial area(s) you had first thought). In fact some of the things you may have written down initially may now appear insignificant compared to the major issues that are jumping off your page.

I can recall a moment in my life when I was feeling overwhelmed and frightened, so I grabbed a pen and paper and did this exact same exercise, recording first the areas that were causing me the most stress, before also recording what emotions I was feeling.

When I wrote a list of the things I thought I was most stressed about, once they were down on paper some of the things were clearly very minor. I was getting myself worked up about them because I wasn't acknowledging the really *big* problem that I was avoiding in my life at that time. On reflection this was the one area that I felt I wasn't able to control.

When you write things down it helps to put them into perspective, so I quickly crossed off some silly things such as 'No food in the fridge' or 'No clean clothes to wear to work tomorrow'. Although I was feeling some stress about these areas the real issue at that time was my relationship, which I had avoided dealing with for some time. I had noted this as the last item on my list of things causing me the most stress, when in fact I realized that it should have been the first.

Have you ever noticed that when you avoid the real *issue*, you begin to worry about *topics* which suddenly get blown out of all proportion. So, for example, you initially may have thought that your stress was being caused by your boss not liking you and giving you a hard time at work; whereas now on reflection you realize that it's not your boss that's the problem, but that you are bored at work and feel unfulfilled. Clearly this is what needs to be dealt with.

Before you start to despair because you've just written a pretty sorry list of everything that needs to change, let me assure you that this *is* a positive, uplifting book and now it's time to turn our attention to the positive aspects of your life and the power of possibility.

Make a wish

By now you'll be very clear about what point you are starting from. You've spent some time thinking about what's not working in your life, and asking yourself the structured questions should have brought to the surface anything that was bothering you deep down. With a clear idea of your starting point, the next step is to realize what this problem area of your life could be like if changed.

When you ask most people what they want, they often spend their time and energy telling you what they *don't* want, instead

WHEN YOU AVOID THE REAL ISSUE, YOU BEGIN TO WORRY ABOUT TOPICS WHICH SUDDENLY GET BLOWN OUT OF ALL PROPORTION.

of what they *do* want! They describe in the greatest detail all the things in their life that are negative – mistakes they've made, the injustices they find themselves in! People tend to be so focused on what they don't want they've no room left to create their ideal future and how they *do* want their life to be!

If you were the pilot of an aircraft and you didn't know your ultimate destination, you'd probably manage to take off at the end of the runway, but all you would end up doing is circling the airfield unclear on which direction to set your course. In the same way, you can't know what action to take unless you know what you are aiming for in life.

Time to change that, starting now! Deciding on what you want is fun, exciting and absolutely your birthright. Remember being a child and writing your Christmas wish list before posting it to the North Pole? Most people dread making decisions about what they want for fear that it won't come true or that others will judge them for their choices. Sometimes we fear deciding on what we want only to discover that it isn't what we wanted after all.

'What if I apply for my dream job and then I don't get it?'

'What if I never find a loving relationship again?'

'I don't have enough money right now, so why even bother dreaming about moving to a bigger house?'

'What if I improve my life and those closest to me stop loving me?'

'What if I train to be a chef and then find I actually don't like it?'

Can anyone guarantee that everything you wish for will come true? Of course not: that also depends on how you go about it and how hard you work for it. But one thing I can guarantee for sure – it definitely won't happen if you don't make that initial choice and decide it's what you really do want. And if it turns out not to be the right thing for you after all, at least you will know and can decide on something else, rather than stay in a place where you are stuck and unhappy.

"Our aspirations are our possibilities."

Dr Samuel Johnson, English writer

Take a look back at the list you made earlier of all the things that you are most concerned about, then spend some time really thinking about the next question.

Question:

What would it be like if this area of your life was perfect?

Record your answers. Some of your wishes maybe tangible and very measureable: this type of house; this particular car; holidays in luxurious parts of the world; earn this amount of money; start a really successful business doing this. However, also pay attention to the feelings that you associate with acquiring these things, as this is where the real truth will lie.

Some of the things on your list may simply be feelings or experiences, or other(s) may be less tangible, more difficult to measure things.

Here is a list of categories that may help you to focus your thinking as you write your wish list.

- Things you may want to acquire.
- Things you may want to learn.
- Experiences you may wish to have.
- Emotions you would like to feel or feel more of.
- Relationships you would like to share.
- Things you would like to create.
- The difference you want to make to someone or something.

Write down everything that pops into your mind – especially if at this stage you have no idea how something could ever be possible.

It's not about the stuff

If you've now got a list of possessions or accoutrements of wealth and you're thinking 'Hang on, I'm not a shallow materialistic person and owning a big house with a swanky car isn't what it's about for me', then you are absolutely right, it shouldn't be.

You are not defined by your circumstances or the stuff you own (unless you choose to be). You are so much more than that. You are defined by who you are, how you behave and the way in which you live your life. There's nothing wrong with having a lovely home, car, lifestyle, etc. but deep lasting fulfilment and happiness comes from within. So when thinking about changes in your life, it's vital that you think about *how you want to feel* as much as what you want to have.

Deciding what you want is only the first step. Next it's really, *really* important to understand what that means to you – emotionally, spiritually and energetically. That's much more important.

DECIDING WHAT YOU WANT IS ONLY THE FIRST STEP. NEXT IT'S REALLY, REALLY IMPORTANT TO UNDERSTAND WHAT THAT MEANS TO YOU.

I recently completed a coaching session with one of my clients who was reviewing his goal board that we had designed six months earlier. It was full of pictures of a fabulous house, a huge office housing his business, a picture of his perfect relationship and he was saying to me, 'But it means nothing Nicola, I feel so disconnected from it all'.

I was able to help him understand that the pictures of his goals were nothing to do with the houses or cars, but what the goals represented emotionally for him. So, for example, the picture of an Aston Martin represented *understated success*, the big office meant *creating employment and reward for hundreds of people*, the yacht represented a particular moment in time when he could *share his success* with his immediate family and friends. Everything was so much more than just the stuff and once he understood that, he was able to reconnect with his goals and therefore his full potential.

So instead of focusing on simply a house, for example, focus on the perfect dwelling where your family can be *safe and protected*. Likewise, instead of focusing on generating £100,000 of new sales revenue in your business in the next four weeks, reframe your goal to *providing an outstanding service for 100 new customers*.

Now we're getting there, even if there is a little part of you saying 'Well, they're only pipe dreams and that's impossible' or perhaps 'If it is that easy, why hasn't it happened yet?'

That's because you need to understand how to break the chain reaction. And that's what we're going to look at in the next chapter.

"The major reason for setting a goal is for what it makes of you to accomplish. What it makes of you will always be the far greater value than what you get."

Jim Rohn, American entrepreneur, author and motivational speaker

SUMMARY

- Every journey starts by defining your starting point.

- Questions always lead to answers: focus on asking the right questions.

- Make a wish by deciding on what you want, rather than how you are going to acquire it.

- Goals are merely the rewards you create for yourself that allow you to feel the emotions you most want in life. So decide what you want to feel and what goals will enable you to feel those emotions even more intensely.

- You are defined not by your circumstances, but by how you lead your life.

02

Breaking the chain reaction – the power of choice

Once you've identified *what* needs to change in your life, it's time to think about *how* to make the change happen. You know that if it was that easy, chances are you would have made the shift by now. That's why it's important to understand *why* you behave in the way you do, and have allowed certain things to happen in your life. We'll then discover how you can 'break the chain reaction' between yourself and anything negative around you.

All of us have automatic responses and behaviours that we use regularly in our lives in response to external events. Sometimes this makes sense – as humans we couldn't possibly think carefully about every single event in a day. It's a very human thing to have automatic responses to certain stimuli – it means you don't have to expend energy in making the same decision every time. So when traffic lights turn red, we stop – without thinking. It makes sense. The problem comes when we have automatic responses in situations where it would be more helpful to *choose* how to react.

Chances are that you have plenty of automatic responses, some of which you probably aren't even aware of. Your automatic response could be to all kinds of stimuli. Maybe you always react in a certain way to one-off perceived injustices, such as the guy who steals your parking space, or it could be that you've developed a standard reaction to constant stimuli, such as things that your partner or your boss say to you. The point is that stuff happens all the time and we respond automatically.

THE POINT IS THAT STUFF HAPPENS ALL THE TIME AND WE RESPOND AUTOMATICALLY.

You might be aware of some or all of your automatic responses and behaviours. Then again, you might not. The thing about automatic responses or reactions is that they are so deeply ingrained that you do things without even thinking about them.

Picture yourself going through your life with the 'universe' hovering over your head. You can choose what the universe looks like – say for now it's in the form of a genie. The universe genie is holding a giant baseball bat waiting to whack you over the head at the next opportunity. Something happens – perhaps you unexpectedly get stuck in traffic which makes you late and this makes you agitated and angry. The universe genie has in fact just given you a hard whack over the head with the baseball bat and is now laughing, 'Ha ha! You're stuck in traffic and now you feel all agitated and angry . . . how bad does that feel?'

Whack! Now you spill coffee down your front: 'Ha ha, ruined! See how frustrated you feel now!'

Whack! Your partner has forgotten to pick up milk on the way home: 'Ha ha, see nobody listens to you or cares what you say', and so on.

With the universe genie hovering over you in this way, you are completely at the mercy of all the events that unfold.

And it's not just the bad things that 'happen to you' if you live your life this way. You are also only allowing yourself to feel positive emotions when positive stimuli come along.

Whack! You close a cracking sale at work: 'Woo hoo, now you feel amazing don't you?'

Whack! You receive a pay rise: 'See, others do appreciate you!'

Whack! He sends you flowers: 'Yee ha, he really does love me!'

If you always live your life in this way, you are always going to be at the mercy of the events around you. There's no chance of choosing how you feel – it's predetermined by the programme running in your head. So often this is exactly what happens. We react unchecked to the stimuli in our environment. And this can be extremely disempowering. The more unchecked our responses are, the more we perceive we are powerless to change them. *But it doesn't have to be this way*.

It is possible to react to the pleasurable stimuli in your life, yet also choose positive reactions to negative stimuli by learning to retrain your *stimulus responses*.

A stimulus response is a learned behaviour. At some point you learned to do it and therefore you can unlearn it and replace it with a more empowering, life-enhancing behaviour. The key to this, is understanding *why* you do it.

You act the way you feel

Now you're thinking about it, you'll probably start noticing your stimulus responses. You're likely to be able to see how when certain things happen, you find yourself responding in a certain way – even when you know it's not the best way to react. And yet you almost can't help yourself – even when you can predict the consequences.

You're meeting your brother. He's late, and you're irritated by it. He finally arrives and you're short with him – your irritation is obvious. He gets defensive and is tetchy in return. The whole situation escalates and nobody benefits. You behave in a tetchy way, because his lateness made you feel tetchy. Your emotions have changed in response to an external stimulus.

Next time you're meeting and again he's later than he said he'd be. You react in exactly the same way and the same pattern unfolds. The more times the pattern is repeated the more deeply ingrained your reactions become, until even the mention of your brother makes you feel tetchy, or you begin to feel tetchy when somebody completely different is only one minute late. Your tetchy emotions and subsequent behaviour have become a *disempowering* stimulus response, now reacting unchecked in many areas of your life.

So how do we see when we have developed stimulus responses that need to be changed? The answer is simple. If behaving in the way you're behaving doesn't help or serve you or the situation, and particularly if your actions are inappropriate, then it's definitely time to do something about it. Remember, in order to behave in a particular way you have to feel that way as well, so why on earth would you want to continue to feel all those negative emotions?

Have you ever been drawn into an argument with someone where you have ended up completely losing your temper and afterwards you don't feel any better – in fact you often feel

REMEMBER, IN ORDER TO BEHAVE IN A PARTICULAR WAY YOU HAVE TO FEEL THAT WAY AS WELL.

worse: the emotion has left you shaken? This is a classic example of where it's important to learn how to break the chain reaction of a negative stimulus and response. And the key to breaking the chain reaction lies at the next level down – the driver of your behaviour.

What's driving you?

Within us all lies an extremely powerful force: the desire to fulfil our emotional needs. Simply put, your emotions drive your behaviour which in turn leads to your experience of life. You act the way you feel.

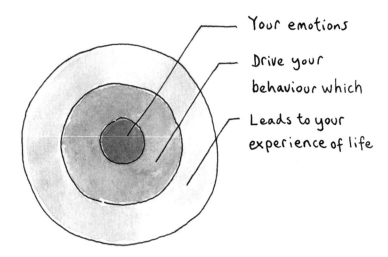

Your emotions

Drive your behaviour which

Leads to your experience of life

So what *are* the emotions that are driving your behaviour? It's a simple question but one that we rarely ask. Most of us spend all our energy focusing on our results, or usually the lack of them. Chances are that until now you've not even been fully aware of how your behaviour creates your life experience, never mind analysed the emotions that are lying beneath.

Well it's time to change that, as being this honest with yourself will give you a real opportunity to find new ways to fulfil your emotional needs. Every emotion you feel, whether positive or negative, whether you are consciously choosing to feel that way, or you are reacting unchecked with a pre-programmed stimulus response, *will* be driving your behaviour. And ultimately it's the way *you* behave that creates *your life*. So if you don't like your life, or some part of it, then you need to recognize that those situations are created by you, your actions and your feelings.

Everything we feel creates results, just not always the results we had hoped for.

Find your driving emotions

To improve any area of your life, then, you need to change your behaviour and to do that you must first change your emotions – how you feel – and how you fulfil your emotional needs. In order to do that, you need to uncover the real reasons why you act the way you do. This can be a bit of a challenge, particularly if it's the first time you've even recognized that you have a choice over how you behave! So let's do a simple exercise to help you uncover the driving emotions in your life.

Think back over the past seven days and write down the five events that led you to have the most intense, positive emotional responses. Then do the same for the five most negative responses. For each event, make a note of how you behaved and then see if you can work out what you think the driving emotion was. Just before you actually do this exercise, remember the emotions you feel as a *result* of your actions are not the same as the *driving emotions* that cause your behaviours. Your *driving emotions* are what you *want* to feel, and by behaving the way you do, at a deep psychological level, you hope to create these feelings, even if the way in which you achieve them is ultimately disempowering you.

For example, everyone knows that they shouldn't overeat. It's clearly unhealthy and can ultimately lead to major health issues. So why do people find it difficult to control their eating? Simply because by eating they unconsciously hope to *feel* something. The same applies to all inappropriate behaviour: you only behave that way because it makes you feel something that you're lacking in.

Common driving emotions

Here are some examples of the most common driving emotions.

- A sense of belonging or being accepted by others.
- A sense of being important and therefore being worthy.
- A sense of being able to control the situation and ultimately your world.
- A desire to be loved.
- A desire for change or new experiences.
- A sense of purpose or fulfilling the needs of a higher force.
- A desire to learn and become better at something.

So take a few moments now and have a think about your most recent behaviours, both those that you know are positive and the ones that are not so good and you know deep down inside do not serve you. Then decide why it is that you behaved in that way – what was the trade-off? Remember, even if the behaviour was inappropriate the driving emotion was probably pure.

I recently spent an intense coaching session with a client who was feeling very overwhelmed and frustrated with the behaviour of a number of members of her team. She simply couldn't understand why they appeared to be 'dropping her in it' left, right and centre, and she felt she had to keep picking up the pieces and solving all their problems. By doing this excercise we were able to recognize that the driving emotion for her was 'control'. Whilst everyone followed her instructions, exactly to the letter, everything was fine; but the moment they deviated from her ideal, then her desire to control the situation became overwhelming and she would do whatever it took to regain that feeling of control – even acting inappropriately.

Another common behaviour that I come across regularly is played out by the person who appears to be extremely generous with their time, expertise and money. On the surface they come across as someone who always wants to help, being everybody's best friend. However, their driving emotion can be a feeling of 'belonging', so the moment others do not appreciate their actions, or they are not invited to a social event, their behaviour changes to being jealous, resentful and even spiteful. All because someone didn't appreciate their efforts and return their actions in a way which gave them a sense of belonging.

Now complete the exercise, and as you recognize your inappropriate behaviour, think about what you were hoping to feel as you acted in that way. The more intense the behaviour the more intense is the desire to feel the driving emotion.

When you made your wish list in Chapter 1, what were the emotions you recorded? Now look back at the original stressors you wrote down and reflect on your behaviour in those areas of your life. *What were you hoping to gain emotionally by behaving in that way?* Ask yourself this question and say the answer out loud or write down what comes into your head. Pay close attention to the language you use, as the answers will very often appear without you even realizing it.

I suspect that the life you desire and the life you are currently experiencing are not the same. And here's the conundrum. Many people make the mistake of desiring outcomes and behaving in a way which they *believe* will make them a better, happier, more fulfilled human being, whereas the reality is that first you need to find more empowering ways to fulfil your actual needs: i.e. the driving emotions you are currently fulfilling through your current disempowering behaviours.

For example, I once worked with a person who listed 'a desire for change and taking risks' as a very important emotional need within her. Yet at a time when she was experiencing change and taking risks in abundance (a time of high uncertainty), she was feeling the most stress! So actually what was more important to her was a feeling of security and certainty. Once she had that emotional need fulfilled, then and only then would she seek the change and risks in her life.

Another client told me that his key driver was 'unconditional love' yet his current behaviour demonstrated that in fact his key driver was a need to 'control' everyone and everything in his life – only then was he able to allow himself to love unconditionally.

What happens if you're in a situation where you don't have your needs fulfilled by the behaviour of others? That's when very often you'll find yourself acting out of impulse, feeling over-whelmed or out of control. Your desire to fulfil your emotional drivers escalates, leading to even more intense behaviour, which is very often inappropriate and usually does not serve you. That's when it's definitely time to do something different.

After all, the best definition of a fool is a person who does the same thing over and over again yet expects to get a different result!

When you find yourself trying to manipulate your environment and people around you to fulfil your own emotional needs, then you are disempowering yourself. You actually have *less* power to change the situation. It's much more empowering to stay

FIRST YOU NEED TO FIND MORE EMPOWERING WAYS TO FULFIL YOUR ACTUAL NEEDS.

focused on your own behaviour and feelings rather than focus on how others affect you.

Deep down you know that this type of disempowering behaviour does not ultimately feel good, so why behave like that in the first place? It's just because you haven't yet learned the techniques to be able to change your behaviour to fulfil all your driving emotions with only empowering behaviours.

There is no right or wrong – it just is, and knowing this about yourself is vital to help you regain your self-control. Now you have worked out what your emotional needs are, I'm going to show you how you can fulfil them in ways that serve you and those around you.

Self-serving vs. selfishness

As you reflect on your actions and behaviours and your driving emotions, you may have realized that behaviours that you have previously believed to be completely selfless are in fact selfish because you receive a trade-off in the form of fulfilling a driving need.

So let me at this stage point out the difference between being selfish and self-serving. Regardless of what others may believe, *the* most important person in the world is YOU! And if you do not do whatever it is to fulfil your own needs first, particularly your driving needs, then you won't be very much use to others.

For example, I meet many people, particularly women, who change completely after having a child. There is no doubt that having a child is a life-changing event in anyone's book, but the danger is when your life *only* becomes about fulfilling the needs of your child. You dangerously shift the centre of your universe and you 'unselfishly' do everything in your power to fulfil your child's needs.

Now obviously as a parent you should be ensuring your child's needs are met, but not at the detriment of your own health and emotional wellbeing. That's why you need to be the centre of your own universe, otherwise you risk being pulled off-centre.

No one is just a parent – you are also an individual, a partner, a son or daughter, perhaps a sibling, a friend, an employee, perhaps a boss, and a raft of other roles. When one of the areas in your life becomes unbalanced, you are in danger of losing the 'whole' you.

My philosophy is that you should *always* fulfil your own needs first, serve yourself first, which is completely different from being selfish. Imagine yourself as a lightbulb. When you are fully filled up you shine brightly and can see for miles, but others are also able to bask in your light. If you don't look after yourself and do what you need to do to keep your light shining, you will become dull and eventually extinguish. You will have nothing left to give. Then in order to see where you are going you have to rely on the light of others, in effect stealing their energy.

This is exactly what happens to parents who don't look after themselves. Eventually they have given of themselves unconditionally for so long that they are totally dependent on the affection and love of their child in return: they rely on their child's light to see where they themselves are going. They have denied themselves everything for so long that if their child is not able to return the affection they crave then they become less tolerant and place conditions on their child's behaviour. They start to live their lives through their child's, in effect using their child's light because theirs has become so depleted.

You can only be the best parent, lover, partner, friend, family member, employee and role model if you look after yourself and put your own needs first.

"Fit your own oxygen mask first."

Amanda Morpeth, international holistic business consultant

You may think that this is an uncomfortable school of thought, but trust me: when you are truly fulfilled in yourself, fulfilling all your driving emotional needs by the choices you make and the way you behave, you will have so much more to give to the world that you will receive even more fulfilment than you could have ever imagined.

However, this may mean that you need to make some different choices now. You may need to learn to say no, and that initially may feel uncomfortable, especially if up until now your natural behaviour has always been to say yes. Accepting every opportunity has been fulfilling a driving emotion within you, perhaps a need to belong, or a need to be accepted, or a need for recognition. Well, no more!

When I first applied this philosophy in my life, it initially caused a bit of tension. Some people found it difficult to accept that I wasn't rejecting *them* when I turned down an invitation – I just knew that my immediate needs meant that I needed to say no to the offer. If I didn't use that time to rest, prepare for a big presentation or get well so that I was 100 per cent fighting fit, then ultimately I would then give less – my light would have been just a bit dimmer.

I still don't always get this right however. It can be tough, especially when you have a driving need to serve others, as many people do. I recently volunteered my time at an event which was important to me, only to arrive completely exhausted and feeling very under par. Every instinct had been telling me to give it a miss, but my need to belong as well as my desire to serve had pushed me on and I falsely believed that once I arrived at the event the adrenaline would carry me through. To say I crashed and burned was an understatement. I spectacularly crashed and burned, ending up doing the one thing that I had wanted to avoid in the first place – I let people down. All because I didn't look after myself first. A better decision would have been to politely excuse myself from the event and take the time I needed to bring my energy back up to par, allowing me to be the best person I can be, in all the areas of my life, as opposed to just one event.

Regain your power

Here's the good news – it doesn't have to be like this. The first part of changing anything is first to acknowledge what needs to be different. Once you've achieved that you'll find everything else in this book is designed to give you multiple strategies to change your life experiences, to reconnect with the power of your possibility and allow the New You to emerge. The next step is to fully own your emotions and therefore your emotional responses.

The ability to feel emotion is part of what makes us human, yet many people think that choosing our emotions or how we feel is beyond our control. However the latest research from Boston University's Center for Memory and Brain, led by Takeo Watanabe, looked at how the brain responds to subliminal stimuli. Researchers recorded not only the responses to the stimuli during the tests, but also how the participants' brains changed as a result of the stimuli. Their findings concluded that the brain, which had long been thought to be unchangeable past infancy, remains impressionable well into adulthood. This means that 'emotions' are in fact *learned,* which ultimately means that if they were originally learned behaviour, then we have the power within us to *learn* new ones. Fantastic news for anyone wanting to change who they are, or something about their life – proof indeed that a leopard really can change its spots.

But this can be difficult. You may be thinking, 'Hang on a minute, I don't choose to be angry, I don't choose to be sad, I don't choose to be lonely', or any of the other emotions you noted down on your earlier list. Well I've got news for you . . . oh yes you do! Nobody forces you to feel or do *anything.* You have the power to choose how you respond to any given stimulus in your life and in your world. Even though we can't control everything that happens to us, we can *always* choose how we respond. You can't change the weather, only how you feel about it, just as you can't control the emotions and behaviours in others, only how you respond to them. This doesn't mean that you don't have any emotional reactions, but that you choose ones that serve you, i.e. ones that ultimately help you move closer to your wish list and make you feel good.

"There is no such thing as the wrong type of weather only the wrong type of clothes, so put on a sexy rain coat and go jump in the puddles!"

Billy Connolly, comedian and writer

No matter how awful an experience you go through or how much pain or negative emotion you feel, you can always choose to deal with it in a way that empowers you and ultimately makes you feel better. When you allow yourself to get stuck in a disempowering behaviour or negative emotion the main person affected is YOU!

When you offer someone a gift, if they choose not to accept it, who does the gift then belong to? That's right, it's still yours – and emotions work in exactly the same way. When you feel negative emotions, at best the only impact they have is on you, at worst you affect others (particularly if they haven't yet had the opportunity to learn what you are learning right now!). They then pass the negativity on to others and it spreads like a cancer, setting off a negative chain reaction.

So when you feel angry because someone has done you an injustice, the main person that the anger affects is you. If the anger does not serve you by, for example, propelling you to take positive action, and instead you get 'stuck' in the negative feeling, then don't hang on to it . . . choose to feel something different.

The challenge with our society is that we've become so focused on what other people have done to us, and the injustices we've been exposed to, that we immediately make ourselves into victims. I describe a victim as someone who does not take responsibility for the emotions they feel. That way, they do not have to take any responsibility for themselves. In order to be truly empowered we have to take 100 per cent full responsibility for ourselves – and that begins by taking control of our emotions.

I remember a conversation with my good friend Kate, who at the time was very heavily pregnant with her first child. The previous day a burst water pipe in the roof of their house had flooded every single room, leaving a mountain of damage, a house full of ruined furniture and nowhere to live, just at a time when she was about to give birth. Most people in that stressful situation

YOU HAVE THE POWER WITHIN YOU TO CHOOSE HOW YOU FEEL ABOUT WHAT IS HAPPENING TO YOU.

would feel overwhelmed and probably a raft of negative emotions including anger, despair and possibly some sadness. Not Kate. Instead, as we were talking, tears of laughter were rolling down my face as she explained her predicament. When I said, 'You seem to be handling this drama pretty damn well, my friend', she responded, 'Well, I made a choice. Being furious won't change the fact that we are living in the aftermath of a flood. We would just be furious and still living in the aftermath of a flood. So instead I'm choosing to see the funny side as it makes me feel stronger and better equipped to get on and deal with it.' Now that's regaining your power!

No matter what your situation appears to be now, you have the power within you to choose how you feel about what is happening to you.

Power questions

Power questions are one of the techniques to use when you need to challenge your feelings, or reframe your emotions about a particular person or situation. Remember, questions always lead to answers and they are a great way of recapturing your power in the moment. Ultimately the end goal is to behave in a way that is empowering and that will serve you and those around you – so here are some of my favourites.

What can I learn from this experience?

No matter what the experience, this question allows you to focus on what you can learn from it so that you can choose a different response next time.

My husband Kevin came into our bedroom one morning as we were both getting ready for work. He had been ironing a shirt downstairs and I could tell from the expression on his face that something was up. 'Do you know when your day can't get any worse and then it does?' was his opening line. Clearly something major had happened. He then went on to explain how he had first plugged the iron into the electrical socket and left it on the carpet to heat up whilst he returned to the cupboard to retrieve the ironing board. On his return to our living room, he discovered that the cat had walked past the iron, knocking it over so that the hotplate was now in contact with the floor. To his horror even in the short space of time he'd been out of the room the hot iron had melted into the carpet, causing permanent damage.

Now I expect most people reading this book at this point are probably thinking the same thing I was at the time: 'You complete idiot, who would leave a hot iron on the carpet, even for a second? You could have burnt the house down, let alone burnt a hole in the carpet!' As he explained the sequence of events I stood stock, feeling the anger begin to bubble. I could feel my heart start to race, my skin go hot and my face burn as if I was going to explode. Kevin was also watching my reaction unfold and, judging by the expression on his face, he was also waiting for an explosion.

However, I realized that if I lost my temper it wouldn't change the fact that the carpet was ruined, and actually he hadn't burnt the house down. It was, after all, only a carpet and he was clearly feeling a tonne of remorse. So instead I took a deep breath and said, 'So what did you learn?' – to which Kevin cheekily responded, with a grin on his face, 'Don't do any ironing!' – and then we both laughed.

Yes, I could have lost my temper, and some would say I would have been justified, but it wouldn't have changed the circumstances – and what is more important to me is our relationship. So by choosing to ask a *power question* I was able to choose a more empowering emotion, leading to a better behavioural response, which in turn created a better life experience for both of us at that moment. And as it is, I've told that story thousands of times, so just think how many people would have missed out if Kevin hadn't had a moment of madness and left the iron to heat up on the carpet.

Power questions

Here are some more power questions to help you regain your power.

- I wonder what is happening that I do not yet understand to make that person say that or behave in that way?
- What do I need to be grateful for?
- How can I deal with this moment brilliantly?
- What do I need to forgive?
- Is this serving me?
- What positive experience can I draw from this?
- What empowering decisions do I need to make right now?
- How can I help?
- What positive things do I need to remember about this person?

Reflections are everywhere

One thing to watch out for with any form of insight is that as you become aware of what's going on and how to change it, very often your mind wanders away from yourself to a long list of other people who should be learning this stuff as well!

I recently had a coffee with a client who has had an amazing journey learning and growing over the past three years. There is no doubt that her progress has been nothing more than astounding and she has moved from a very negative place a few years ago, dependent on heavy medication to artificially control her mood, to now feeling totally empowered, in control and much, much happier in all aspects of her life.

However, during the conversation she was very scathing about her boss, saying that although he thought he was a great boss he still had many flaws.

The interesting aspect of the conversation was how much the boss's behaviour was still affecting my client's emotions, even though she felt she was in absolute control of her responses. Obviously, as she was beginning to project her frustrations outwards again, honing in on her boss, it became clear that she was still responding negatively to an external stimulus.

I was able to help her ask herself why, when she was now able to control her emotional responses in many areas of her life, did she still feel so strongly about this particular person's behaviour? And the answer lies in the reflection of that person's behaviour back to us.

We see in others what we need to work on in ourselves. So if you find yourself becoming frustrated with a particular person or their behaviour, rather than focus on what they need to fix or change, always bring the focus back on to yourself and ask a power question such as 'What is it about this person's behaviour that is a reflection of what I need to be aware of in my own behaviour?' The more intense your emotional response, the more powerful the reflection.

So, no matter what the stimulus, remember to take a deep breath and ask a power question to allow you to regain your power in the moment, and choose your emotion and a better way of reacting.

"Eye for an eye will make the whole world blind."

Mahatma Gandhi, spiritual leader

SUMMARY

- Emotions drive behaviour, which in turn leads to your experience of life.

- Regain your power by taking full ownership of everything you feel.

- Often behaviour which we believe to be selfless is in fact selfish. Instead focus on self-serving behaviours that allow your light to shine brightly.

- Use a power question in the moment to regain your self-control.

- When we become fixated on other people's behaviour, it's because it provides a reflection of our own.

03

Who are you? –
the power of authenticity

What is it that makes you unique? You were born with unique gifts and talents which, when you apply them in life, will give you the greatest joy and pleasure and, not surprisingly, the greatest success. So who are you really?

If time and money were no object, what would your life be like: how would you use your talents and gifts? An interesting question, isn't it? And one that allows you to reconnect with your authenticity.

Very often we hide our 'authentic self' behind elaborately created facades. We hide 'the real me' from everyone around us: our partner, our friends, our family and our work colleagues. In doing so, we believe that we will protect ourselves from the judgement and criticisms of others and make ourselves feel better – in that moment at least.

We then build our lives in ways that are very often designed to fulfil the needs and expectations of others, or society at large, all the while burying our authentic self deeper and deeper, until we become so disconnected from that part of ourselves that we even forget who we truly are. We become trapped in a web of expectations rather than being free to live our lives in full alignment with our mind, body and spirit.

Until you rediscover your authenticity you will never be truly fulfilled, successful and happy. You will always have the feeling that you are missing something, that you are stuck or trapped in your situation or have the sinking sensation in the pit of your stomach that simply won't go away.

Go with the flow

Life should be easy and flow effortlessly. The water in a river flows downstream to the sea. Should any obstacles fall across its path the water will flow around or over, consistently moving onwards in its purposeful direction.

When you live authentically this is how life feels – easy, graceful and purposeful. When you do this you enter a state called *flow*. When you move against your authenticity you feel like you are swimming upstream, against the current, and it feels like everything is working against you: it's a struggle.

You've probably heard of the terms 'get into flow' or 'go with the flow' to describe activities that to you feel simple, easy and most importantly enjoyable. And it may be no surprise to know that the feeling of flow isn't just some illusive state of mind that only some people are able to achieve. Understanding this phenomenon, and how we can duplicate it in our own lives, has been the life work of scientist Mihaly Csikszentmihalyi, a professor and former chairman of the Department of Psychology at the University of Chicago.

He concluded that the state of flow appears when an individual achieves the right balance between the level of skill and the level of challenge in any given task. Too high a skill without challenge leads to boredom; too high a challenge without the appropriate skill set leads to anxiety and stress; whereas no challenge or skill required leaves you apathetic and disinterested.

LIFE SHOULD BE EASY AND FLOW EFFORTLESSLY.

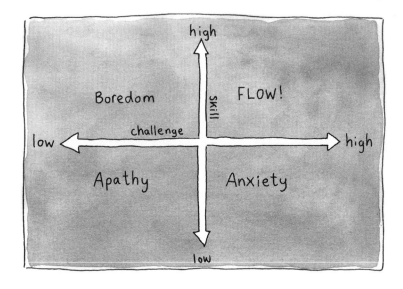

So when do you know you've personally achieved that magical state of flow? Trust me you *will* know. Firstly, you'll really be enjoying yourself and you'll be full of energy and passion for the task you're undertaking. Very often you'll be totally absorbed in what you're doing, unaware of time passing until you come out of flow and are shocked to discover that hours may have passed. Another key trait is that you won't feel any anxiety, stress or fear; you'll be totally in the moment, often unaware even of your own physical body!

Some people even describe this state as a feeling of clarity, peace, ecstasy and a connection with their higher self or intuition. Sounds great, doesn't it!

From this description, you may already know what you're doing when these kind of feelings occur. If not, make a list of all the times in your life when you have been in flow. Below are some examples to get your creative juices flowing. Remember, if time and money were no object, what would you spend your time on?

Many of these activities may appear very broad in their description and you may not have had the opportunity to do them for quite some time. It doesn't matter – write them down anyway.

Examples of flow

- Connecting with people and starting conversations.
- Exercising or playing sport.
- Creative writing.
- Playing with your child.
- Cooking.
- Inventing things.
- Gardening or being in nature.
- Making things.
- Caring for animals.
- Thinking of new ideas.
- Logical thinking or working with numbers.
- Solving problems.

As with every brainstorm, it helps if you are in a high energy state, so take a deep breath in and, if it's possible, stand up. Ask yourself, 'What am I doing when I feel totally absorbed and really at one with what I'm doing?' Do not pre-judge any thoughts that pop into your brain, as it's too easy to dismiss information that can be useful to you, when that little voice inside your head chirps up and tells you, 'Nah don't bother writing that down . . . that's rubbish'. Record everything you can think of, no matter how random, as you can always discount it later.

Did that spark some ideas that perhaps you may not have thought of for quite a long time? Or did you pretty much know the answers straight away? If the latter, then you're already very in tune with your uniqueness and it's likely you are seeking ways to pursue your gifts in your life.

The trick to leading an authentic life is to use your talents and skills to your advantage, and receive the appropriate rewards. Take a moment to look back at the brainstorm you've just done and circle the skills that you possess which you could develop into an income stream or which someone would be willing to pay for. This is where it gets really interesting.

If your list included things like playing professional football (but you're 35), or playing computer games on the Xbox, then let's be realistic. Although these may be activities that you posses some uniqueness in and happen to be really good at, is it realistic that you could turn these talents into an income stream?

However, as you circle the activities on your list, you might find something that could be a real opportunity for you. One of the keys to leading a more successful life is to get paid for doing what you love! Find a job you love doing and you'll never again have to work a day in your life!

Discovering a passion in life

After completing this exercise on a training programme, one delegate realized that her passion in life was and always had been to become a nurse. However her choices had led her down a path where she was married with three lovely children and needed the wage from her current job to contribute to the family income, even though she absolutely hated her work. Her coping mechanism had been to numb herself and become a zombie at work – as that was the only way she could make it through the days. However, clearly this strategy was not adding quality to her life and in fact fighting against her flow was making her tired, so she had no energy left for her family at the end of the day.

Once she understood her authenticity the choice then became easy. It was a long-term commitment, a journey that she undertook beginning with resitting some of her school exams. She studied alongside her family and work until finally, seven years later, she has now achieved her goal of becoming a nurse. Although seven years of hard graft on top of running a home, looking after three children, a marriage and a normal life may seem like a huge commitment to some people, in the bigger scheme of things what is seven years out of the whole of your life, if that will allow you to live the rest of your life authentically?

Has it become blatantly obvious to you that you are simply not using your unique talents enough? Whether you work for yourself, are in employment or support your family domestically, I bet you are wasting many of your talents. As we explained earlier, a life without flow is one that either feels stressful, unchallenging and boring, or one in which you feel apathetic – the worst feeling I would suggest, as this is a life without passion or purpose.

A LIFE WITHOUT FLOW IS ONE THAT EITHER FEELS STRESSFUL, UNCHALLENGING AND BORING, OR ONE IN WHICH YOU FEEL APATHETIC.

Maximize your flow

In order to maximize the flow in your life I suggest that you divide your daily activities into three key areas. The first is your *uniqueness*, which is all the things that we've just discussed, the talents that you possess and the activities in which you can easily achieve flow.

The second I call *stuff* and this includes the tasks that you have to do to survive but which do not enrich your life. So, for example, these could include some domestic chores, or certain functions in your day-to-day job.

And finally the last group I call *energy zappers*. This is the group of activities that you feel obliged to do, but give you no enjoyment and you are likely to be rubbish at. Personally I would put bookkeeping in this category, together with ironing. I hate ironing, or should I say that more positively: I really wish I could like ironing more!

I suggest you aim to build a life that allows you to spend 70 per cent of your time using your uniqueness, 25 per cent of your time doing stuff and only allow 5 per cent (or ideally less) doing tasks and activities that zap your energy. Achieving that kind of balance would not only make you more fulfilled but more productive too.

But how exactly do you make it all happen?

Building an authentic life

Your time is a very valuable resource. You can't make more of it, so the only choice you have is how you choose to use it. Doing things in the middle of the night and sacrificing sleep isn't a long-term, life-enhancing option.

How do you spend your time currently? How much of your day is spent on those activites that you consider to be your unique abilities? How much requires you to deal with stuff? What about time given away to activities that are just zapping your energy? If you were to record an average day in your life, how far away from the ideal of 70:25:5 would you be?

It's possible you are now feeling completely demoralized and thinking 'I'm not spending any time doing what I'm good at. My life is full of stuff and energy zappers and it feels impossible to change it around.' You feel so obligated to your current commitments and current set-up that you don't know how or where to begin making the shift. If so, then start by using the three simple techniques below to redress the balance.

Tip 1: Eliminate the energy zappers and delegate the stuff

Simple in concept but not always easy: however, extremely necessary to allow you to focus on the New You. I understand it might not be practical or affordable to offload *all* the things you don't like doing, but it is worth thinking about what your options are.

Does every task really need to be done? And if so, does it really have to be done by you?

If you really loathe ironing and are hopeless at it, you might decide it's worth paying somebody locally to remove this bugbear from your life. Or to do a deal with a friend who quite enjoys ironing – they do your ironing and in return you do something for them (the gardening, sort out their finances, mend their car, regular baking) – whatever you're good at and they hate. If you can free up time from doing things that get you down, and spend it doing something you are really good at and enjoy, so much the better.

You can also 'delegate' to systems – say delegating incoming phone calls to an answerphone, then return the calls when it suits you, rather than react to every phone call when it happens, especially if you need to be focusing on something more important.

Why not have your grocery shopping delivered to your door? It may cost a little extra, but by delegating the travelling to and from the supermarket to the delivery service as well as the time you would have spent going round the store, you will have saved yourself money on travelling yourself, and most importantly, saved yourself valuable time. Setting up regular deliveries of core items to which you can add extras is hugely time saving.

Tip 2: Outsource to an expert

Think about this: your stuff is likely to be someone else's unique abilities. You may be thinking, 'I would employ someone to do my bookkeeping/ironing if I could afford to'. You need to appreciate that if you were to focus more of your time and energy on your uniqueness, from which you can generate income, you have the potential to increase your earnings, so it's a win/win situation. Also, when your stuff is someone else's uniqueness they are likely to be much more efficient at getting the task done and, remember, it will create flow for them.

Tip 3: Schedule in time for activities that generate flow

Sometimes we just have to be disciplined in ring-fencing time to make sure we give ourselves enough time to do the things we love, especially if they generate income for us. So make a date in your schedule and stick to it.

I guarantee that if you implement these techniques, you will attract to you the people you need to complement your unique abilities, both in your professional and personal life.

By choosing to be more productive, by focusing on your uniqueness, which automatically gets you 'into flow', not only will you lead a more fulfilling life but also one that will be more successful.

I haven't found my uniqueness yet

But what if you haven't yet found your unique talents and skills? I would hazard a guess that either you simply haven't had enough life experience yet, or you've been 'stuck' in a life and have become zombified for so long that you have forgotten how to fully engage in living.

If that's the case, then the answer is easy. Get out there and explore. Find ways to try new stuff. Travel to places you've never been to and do things you've never done. Read books, watch interesting TV programmes. Speak to people and all the while pay attention to what you truly enjoy doing. Everyone has something to offer and part of your journey in your life is to discover it, then live it.

If you're really struggling here, realizing that your life is spent on things that you don't enjoy and aren't good at, and you don't know where to start to put it all right, then it's useful to know why you stay in situations and circumstances even when you know they are not working for you. Interestingly, it's because you haven't experienced enough 'pain' yet.

Pain vs. pleasure

If we know what we should be doing, why do we then choose the path of least resistance – knowing that actually we are self-sabotaging ourselves?

For example, we all know that if we eat sensibly and undertake a moderate amount of exercise we will have a healthy body and lots of energy. So why do we scoff an entire packet of biscuits instead of only eating one? Likewise we also intellectually understand that if someone starves themselves and exercises vigorously whilst aiming to achieve their perfect body image, they are very likely to die before ever achieving their ideal of perfection.

So when we know this stuff, why do we still do it? The answer lies again in our driving emotions, which, remember, drive all our behaviours and are the key to our life experience.

Austrian psychiatrist Dr Alfred Alder concluded that there are two driving emotional forces within all of us: feelings of inferiority and feelings of superiority. Pain and pleasure: we are constantly fluctuating to achieve a balance between the two. More simply put, we all want to avoid pain in our lives – obviously physical pain but also emotional pain – and we're also motivated by the desire for pleasure both physically and emotionally. Avoid pain, seek pleasure.

Now most people believe the more influential of these two forces is the desire for pleasure. Think about it, have you ever been told 'Work hard and earn this huge financial bonus', or 'Exercise, lose 5 kilos and you'll feel great', or 'Be nice to your partner and they'll love you for it'? But for many people, perhaps you included, unconsciously this is still not enough to keep you motivated to do the right thing in a sustained way.

PAIN AND PLEASURE: WE ARE CONSTANTLY FLUCTUATING TO ACHIEVE A BALANCE BETWEEN THE TWO.

The human mind is wired to be more motivated to avoid pain than to strive for the *possibility* of pleasure! That is why we *always* take the path of least resistance; we are more motivated by avoiding pain. We will only apply ourselves with the minimum amount of effort required to avoid the consequences that we consider too painful and therefore wish to avoid. This is what I call your *tipping point*.

Think of a child's behaviour. Any parent (especially those of a strong-willed toddler) knows that a child will continuously test the boundaries with their behaviour, until the consequences become too great: then they'll behave. Even if it means you have to put your child back on the 'naughty step' 20 times until the penny drops. 'Ahh … there are consequences for hitting Daddy over the head with my toy tractor.' Providing the consequences (the pain) for doing so, i.e. time out on the naughty step, outweigh the pain of having to modify the behaviour, i.e. finding something

more fun to do than whacking Daddy over the head, the child will choose a different behaviour. And for us adults it's the same.

I can remember when I was a college student and wondering why, when I had six whole weeks to complete an assignment, I always ended up working through the days and nights for the three days before the deadline to get the work completed! Now I understand it was simply because six weeks earlier my perception of the consequences (or the pain) of missing out on a night out, or a string of nights out, with my friends (I was a student – what can I say in my defence!) as opposed to staying home and study, was too great a sacrifice. As the deadline approached, suddenly the greater pain now lay in the consequences of not completing my work! Therefore my motivation changed and although I was still tempted to spend time socializing, hitting my deadline became a higher priority.

Ever wondered why relationships often end over seemingly trivial incidents? Again, it's simply a shift in the pain equation. I know of a couple who split up over a loaf of bread! At the time, one of the parties involved couldn't understand what had happened and felt completely wounded that such a trivial matter could lead to the end of a 15-year relationship. Clearly, however, it wasn't just about a loaf of bread – or lack of it in this case! In that moment the other person had hit their tipping point. It was now more painful for them to stay in the relationship than suffer the consequences of leaving.

These motivators are forming a huge part of your life – right now. In absolutely every decision you make, unconsciously you are deciding which behaviour is going to help you avoid more pain and feelings of inferiority.

If you've ever wondered why someone would choose to stay in a life situation that is clearly causing them pain – for example a job that they hate, or an abusive marriage which they don't change or leave – the answer lies here. In their mind (although these thoughts are likely to be unconscious) the pain and consequences of making changes currently still outweigh the pain of remaining in their current circumstances. Usually they would rather move the responsibility to their stimuli and label themselves as a 'victim', which means that they don't have to accept any responsibility for their circumstances. It becomes just the way things are and they feel powerless to change the circumstances that they *perceive* are outside their control.

Don't get me wrong: I don't believe anyone would consciously choose to put themselves into a painful situation and play the victim, but it least Alfred Alder's work explains why when we live in a world of so much choice, someone would choose *not* to change their circumstances. So if this rings true with you, what do you need to do about it?

Turn up the heat – then get out of the kitchen!

If you are just 'settling for this' in any area of your life, or you are frustrated that you can't stay motivated to behave in more empowering ways, then it's time to turn up the heat. You need *more pain* to avoid.

This doesn't mean, however, that you put yourself in harm's way or physically inflict pain on yourself! What it does mean, however, is that you need to associate *more pain* with not changing and *less pain* with making a positive shift.

Very often we allow our choices in the moment to slide by, justifying them by saying, 'It won't matter in the long run'. Well, it's time to change that focus.

Take your lifestyle choices for example. We know we need to drink 2 litres of water a day, we know we should eat 5 portions of fruit and vegetables and we know we should exercise for 20 minutes 3 times a week. Yet do we all do it? Only you know the answer.

My good friend Dr Fiona Ellis, who is one of the healthiest people I know, has a fantastic question she asks many of her patients: 'Today are you going to dig your grave with your teeth?' That makes you stop and think, as you reach for that extra sticky bun or second bottle of wine.

In order for you to make the shifts you desire, it's necessary to uncover your own tipping point. What would you absolutely *not* accept and how long would you need to *not* make a change before you hit that point in your life? This ultimately is the point where you discover your motivation.

For some people their tipping point may be relatively low. If their jeans suddenly feel a bit tight, or they have to slacken their belt one notch, then that's enough to make them take action to lose those few extra pounds. Or they would absolutely not allow a small tiff in their relationship to fester and they would always make sure they cleared the air before bedtime.

Perhaps they wouldn't allow a negative team situation at work to build up and would take action to nip it in the bud early, ensuring everyone involved understood the boundaries and expectations of their behaviours.

Other people would never allow their bank balance to fall below a certain amount before hitting their tipping point and making different choices in managing their finances.

So, in relation to your life and your choices, let's take a couple of examples and ask some questions that will help you work out your personal tipping point and find where you reach the point of self-motivation.

- **Overspending.** How much debt would you have to accumulate before you stopped spending? Would you have to lose your house, making your family homeless? Perhaps when the bailiffs knocked on your door and took the TV and your children's toys, that would be the moment for you? Maybe having to ask for money from a family member or friend would be the worst-case scenario? Or is it simply that you wouldn't allow your bank balance to fall below a certain amount?

- **A far from perfect relationship**. Would the time to change be the moment when either of you start to use character assassination, name calling or verbal abuse when you become frustrated? Maybe things would have to become physically abusive, or one or both of you would have looked outside the relationship to have your needs met? Or do you respond the minute you and your partner become disconnected even for a few hours?

- **Unhealthy and overweight**. Would your tipping point come by just seeing your less than attractive holiday photographs, or not being able to walk up the stairs without feeling out of breath? Or perhaps you would have to develop a serious, life-threatening illness before you would take action? Or would it just be not being able to fit into your favourite pair of jeans?

One of the most powerful ways to associate more pain with not changing now is to project forward into your future – maybe 1, 5 or 10 years hence or even longer – and imagine what your life would be like if you didn't make the shift now. For many people just simply being in the same situation further into their future is enough to do it: imagine still being overweight in a year's time, or not being financially secure, yet being 10 years older. How would that feel?

Very often the challenges in our lives become more serious the longer we go on ignoring them. So, if you do this exercise for yourself and suddenly you appreciate that if you don't make the small changes now, your life would be *more* painful 10 years down the line, then you now have massive motivation to make those shifts, today.

Now let's discover two ways you can sustain this new-found motivation and drive.

1 Perk up your Scooby ears

One of the areas you need to master is to understand the impact of your behaviour on your life. Are you getting closer to where you want to be? Or are you moving further away, or, as I like to call it, 'using your Scooby ears'?

As a child I was a huge fan of the cartoon *Scooby Doo*. The plot always followed the same format and reached a point where Shaggy was being dragged backwards into a cupboard by the Ghost, which was in fact the Caretaker in disguise! (I was about 10 years old when I sussed that one out.) Anyway, at this exact point in the plot, Scooby would prick up his ears and make his trademark Scooby grunt as he tried in vain to alert the other members of the gang to the impending danger. In that moment Scooby Doo 'got it'. His sensory acuity was telling him something was up.

Using your Scooby ears simply means using all of your senses to become much more aware of your environment or, to use the technical term, using your 'sensory acuity'. This is a gift that all animals, including humans, have. Yet very often we are so focused on ourselves that we don't read the signals that are all around us.

Boxing Day 2004 is a day that will always be remembered for the tragic tsunami in the Indian Ocean which claimed hundreds of thousands of lives in countries as far apart at Sri Lanka, Thailand, the Maldives and Somalia. Following the tragedy it was widely reported that many animals began to behave

VERY OFTEN WE ARE SO FOCUSED ON OURSELVES THAT WE DON'T READ THE SIGNALS THAT ARE ALL AROUND US.

strangely just before the tsunami hit land, all desperate to move to higher ground. In fact in Sumatra a herd of tamed elephants broke their chains in their bid to reach safety before the waves came. The elephants were able to use their senses, feeling the vibrations of the incoming waves through their feet, which alerted them to the impending danger.

However, many of us humans often drift through our days missing all the signals that are around us. By simply tuning into your Scooby ears you are able to become much more aware of the impact of your actions both in the short and long term – helping you discover your tipping point much, much earlier. Maintaining motivation then becomes so much easier.

Some people also describe this as being *in the present*. It's an intention to be more aware of your environment and your impact on it. So whether you are interacting with another person or are on your own, pay attention to the impact your behaviour has on your environment. When you do this, *you* have now become the stimulus, just as if you were to toss a pebble into a pool of water, generating the ripples that radiate outwards from the entry point.

When you tune up your Scooby ears and fully participate in your world, the changes you make internally through your emotions, and outwardly through your behaviours, have a far greater impact, and your Scooby ears are your feedback mechanism that allows you to then evaluate your results. And if you're not getting the response you hoped for, or in fact needed, then it's time to apply some behavioural flexibility.

2 Behavioural flexibility

Life is never a straightforward journey. Even if you know your starting point, have your pin firmly planted in your map, know exactly where you want to be, are in control of your emotional responses and are totally motivated to do whatever it takes to achieve your success (i.e. the pain of not doing it is much too great) – even then you still don't have the guarantee of a smooth and easy passage!

That's where behavioural flexibility becomes crucially important. The term *behavioural flexibility* means exactly that: being flexible in how you behave. If you only have one way of achieving your outcome, what happens if that stops working? Unless you're flexible in your approach, you're left with no alternatives.

Suppose you drive to work via the same route every day and one day the road is unexpectedly closed. You have two options: complain and grumble about the fact that the road is closed, or be flexible, get on and find an alternative route.

What do you do in your business when your best customers take their business elsewhere, leaving a big hole in your order book? Or when your relationship hits a rocky patch? Or you have a sudden squeeze on your finances? Do you use your Scooby ears to recognize that events have taken a different direction and you are now moving further away from your ideal, and then you apply some behavioural flexibility to do whatever it takes to get back on track? Or do you keep doing what worked in the past and then complain or play the 'victim' when things don't work out?

Suppose your relationship has suddenly hit a rocky patch. Even if you don't believe you've contributed to the situation, if you recognize that the relationship has gone downhill, and are clear that you want it to be fulfilling and rewarding again, you have an opportunity to do something about it by changing your behaviour. What worked before, clearly isn't working now. So you can decide to complain endlessly to your friends about how things aren't the same as they were, or how it's your partner's fault, or you can try new ways of behaving until your partner responds in the positive manner you want. And if the changes in your approach don't work immediately, then keep using your behaviourial flexibility – *until* you get the response you want.

"We haven't failed. We know a thousand things that won't work, so we're that much closer to finding what will."

Thomas Edison, American inventor

If it's important enough to you, you'll keep changing your approach in any situation, until you get the outcome you want. The parents of a disabled child often won't accept a doctor's opinion if they are told, 'Your child will never walk'. They will continue to encourage their child and do whatever it takes to support their child's desire for mobility. Although the child may not walk in the conventional sense, they *will* usually find a way to get around the problem.

The one thing you can always guarantee in life is that just when you think you've got it cracked, the universe will pop along with its great big baseball bat and give you another whack just to check that you're paying attention. That's when the person with the most behavioural flexibility will *always* achieve their outcome first!

So whatever your desired goal, think about the many different ways you can behave that are going to help you achieve your desired outcomes.

I love the British TV programme *Supernanny* with Jo Frost. The scenario is always the same: a family with children who are behaving completely inappropriately call in Supernanny for help. When she arrives on the doorstep, she is greeted by one or two worn-out parents who usually begin by exclaiming 'They just won't behave and we've *TRIED EVERYTHING!*'

They haven't *really* tried everything of course, and all Supernanny does is get stuck in with her box of tricks, using multiple tried and tested ways of getting the children to behave. She simply has *more* behavioural flexibility. She has *more* strategies to get the children to behave appropriately than they have strategies to misbehave. The impact is immediate: often in only a few hours she is able to help the family and re-establish harmony in the household.

So if you're frustrated and you feel that you've run out of options to deal with certain areas in your life, particularly when previously everything was going fine, then remember there are always more options. Your job is to find them. Never forget there will be another route, another way, another answer. It's just that you haven't thought of it yet. When you're really struggling, try asking yourself a power question: 'What other way is there of doing this?' You'll be surprised what you can come up with.

SUMMARY

- Everyone is born with unique skills and talents which when applied lead to a more fulfilling life.

- Focus on your unique abilities, delegate the stuff and remove the energy zappers.

- You reach your tipping point when you associate more pain and consequences with *not* changing than with making a change.

- Perk up your Scooby ears and use behavioural flexibility to tune into your surroundings and keep a check on your results.

04

Your perception = your reality – the power of changing your focus

When you wear sunglasses, it instantly changes your perception of what you see, especially if the sunglasses have coloured lenses. If the lenses are blue, for example, not only is your world tinted blue, but the blue in your vision appears even more pronounced.

This is true of all the filters through which you see and experience your world. They tint your view and make certain things seem more pronounced. You see your world through many filters, but with most you don't even know they exist.

I'm sure everyone has experienced that moment at the end of a relationship when a trusted friend comments, 'Well, we could never see what you saw in him/her'. At the time you're feeling dejected and wounded: 'Thanks for that,' you think, 'that's so helpful right now – not!' Yet it's so telling. When you first enter a relationship you are so in love that your focus is on how amazingly wonderful that person is, to such an extent that you are completely unaware of any shortcomings. In fact, because you are consciously focusing on all their good points your brain filters out any annoying habits. You are simply not aware of them.

It's only once the 'honeymoon period' has passed and you shift your focus that you become more aware of their less-endearing habits. Suddenly the way they hold their fork becomes a big deal. You've removed the 'rose tinted' glasses and now you are seeing them in full colour.

YOU SEE THE WORLD THROUGH MANY FILTERS, BUT WITH MOST YOU DON'T EVEN KNOW THEY EXIST.

However, as a relationship progresses sometimes we start to focus more and more on our partner's annoying habits and shortcomings. If you're not careful you will apply a *negative filter* where all your awareness is now on how annoying they are. You completely delete any of their good points.

The good news is that there is a reason for this – and once we understand it, this is another area of our psychology we can use massively to our advantage to support the New You.

Sunglasses for your brain

Our nervous systems, and ultimately our brains, are being bombarded every second of every day with millions and millions of messages and signals from every sensory receptor in our bodies. However, our brains work much faster than we can consciously think, so in order for us to make sense of our world our brains use three coping mechanisms to help us create order and allow us to interact with the world around us. These brain filters work just the same as if you were wearing a set of sunglasses with tinted lenses.

We sort the incoming signals by:

- *generalizing* and grouping information together
- *distorting* the information – bending the truth to fit into our perception
- *deleting* the information completely from our awareness.

Let me give you some examples of each one. You walk into a room for the first time, say at a restaurant. At the moment you reach the door, unless you've previously opened *that* particular door, you have no historical references in your memory to instruct you how to open the door; yet you do it seamlessly – how? You don't have to stop, analyse the door and try out a number of strategies on how to open it. You use other similar past experiences from your life of opening thousands of doors to quickly interpret the information that is being received into your brain. You *generalize* the information and make an assumption on the strategy you need to apply in order to open that particular door. In fact, you are so efficient at doing this, unless you encounter a problem, say for example the door is locked, you are likely to be able to perform this simple task unconsciously without even thinking about it. This is an example of your brain generalizing information to allow you to quickly interpret a lot of information and take the appropriate action swiftly and efficiently.

Body image is a good example of how some people *distort* information. A 1997 survey in *Psychology Today* reported that 56 per cent of women and 40 per cent of men have a distorted negative perception of their own body image, i.e. they believe they are fatter or have a bigger nose or whatever, than they really have. For these people, even though they are seeing what everybody else sees and receiving the same signals that others receive, they are *distorting* the image to 'fit' with their self-perceptions. They are applying a negative body image filter to themselves and until they change the filter it is almost impossible for them to long-term change their habits. It's also possible to have positive distortions. I often wonder how it is possible that I can look in the mirror and think I look pretty good – then fail to fit into my favourite pair of jeans!

Finally, we *delete* information all the time without even realizing it. If you've ever seen a master magician at work, they use distraction techniques as a way of controlling your focus so that they can create their illusions. Very often the trick happens right under your nose, yet because you *delete* the signals you are 'surprised' and entertained when they reveal their magic.

What this means ultimately is that we shape our world, or at least our *perception* of our world, based on the filters we apply. Therefore our own perception equals our own reality, our life experience and ultimately the quality of life we lead.

Are you a Tigger or an Eeyore?

You need to decide if you're going to be a Tigger or an Eeyore. Both characters from the tales of Winnie-the-Pooh (written by A.A. Milne) live in the same world and embark on the same adventures. However, based on their perceptions of their world they have very different life experiences.

Tigger bounces through life always perceiving the fun in things, the possibility of what could be, how problems can be solved and the fact that everything will eventually turn out alright. Eeyore, on the other hand, is the complete opposite. He always perceives the negatives, and assumes everything will go wrong. Eeyore never takes chances and when things sometimes do take a turn for the worse he always points out, 'I told you so'. In fact Eeyore is so gloomy that a little rain cloud forms above his head and follows him everywhere! And he blames the cloud for most of the things that happen to him, perceiving that all the doom and gloom is inevitable.

If you find yourself living under a cloud then maybe it's time to inject a bit of Tigger's bounce into your life.

"It'll be alright in the end, if it's not alright then it's simply not the end – yet."

Kate Spencer, health and wellbeing consultant

Very often we apply negative filters to those who are closest to us, which is why we often bicker with our nearest and dearest. Have you ever seen red, just because your loved one has left a few unwashed dishes on the side, or because they take the wrong turning on a car journey, or because they feed the children chocolate just before dinner ... or a million other little things that seem *so* important at the time that you find yourself becoming disproportionately frustrated? If so, then you definitely need to change your filter. That's when reinjecting some of the original rose tint from when you first met won't do any harm. Instead of focusing on your partner's bad points, remind yourself of some of their more charming qualities.

The same applies to anyone who you find getting under your skin, particularly if the things that are irritating you are essentially small stuff.

Filter your past to see differently in the present

Every experience we have in life is filed away in our brains and becomes the framework against which we recall information to assess our current circumstances.

When we go through life on a day-to-day basis we use the three methods of generalizing, distorting and deleting information to create our understanding of a situation and we base our assumptions on past experiences that we've filed away.

So, for example, in the previous scenario of opening a door, because we have had so many experiences in our past of opening doors, we use the memories to very quickly assess our current situation and make a decision as to the appropriate course of action to take.

The more emotion, positive or negative, attached to the memory, the stronger the memory becomes etched on our brains. Which is why, often when we have had a negative experience in our lives, if at the time we had an intense emotional reaction to that event, that memory often lies close to the surface of our consciousness. If we are not careful this can cause us to create a filter of our current reality which is also very negative. But rather than living like Eeyore, always under a cloud, you can change your filter instead!

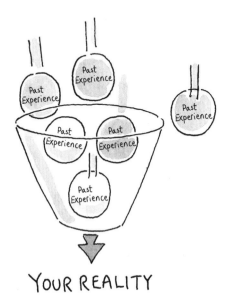

YOUR REALITY

We can't change our past, it's done, gone and there is absolutely nothing we can do to undo it. We can only learn from our past experiences and use that information to make different choices in the present. This decision alone is enough to make the smallest of changes in the New You that over time will lead to a very different future.

When we think of 'the past' we often recall information from a significant time ago, but don't forget that the past is also only a few weeks, days, hours and moments ago. So if you are frustrated about something that happened only a few hours ago, remember to reframe the meaning you associate with those events by asking an appropriate power question.

Just like choosing our responses to any stimuli, we also have the power to chose our memories, or at least the meaning we associate with those experiences – no matter how painful or negative they may have seemed at the time.

Release the past with joy

If as you are reading this section you recognize some events, people or circumstances that you still feel negative about, then you need to let them go. Holding on to that negative emotion is only providing more fuel to create a negative current reality, which in turn creates more negative memories to add into the mix – and so the cycle continues.

Deciding to forgive whatever it is, and I mean truly forgive, has only positive benefits for you. It empowers you, allows you to move forward in your life and gives you the power to create your own life experience. Forgiving does not mean that you have to condone the actions of that person or situation, but simply that you accept that the things that happened happened, and you are choosing not to allow them to affect you any more.

One of the most painful emotional experiences of my life was the end of my first marriage. At the time I felt very much a victim that had been 'hard done by' and to say I was heart-broken was an understatement. At the time every aspect of my life was affected – my health, my job, my social circle and my friends, my finances, both our families. Anyone who has been

DECIDING TO FORGIVE WHATEVER IT IS, AND I MEAN TRULY FORGIVE, HAS ONLY POSITIVE BENEFITS FOR YOU.

through a similar experience will appreciate how upsetting a divorce can be.

At the time I felt very much the wounded party as I wanted to work things out, yet it was clear that we had developed very different goals which were literally pulling us apart to opposite ends of the world. So we decided to separate.

Because I had seen myself as the victim I held on to that pain for over two years. Almost all my conversations would end up reverting back to this subject and how unfair life was. I was 'stuck' in the divorce even though time was moving on. I didn't know how to move past this experience until I realized I needed to release my past with joy.

From that moment on, every time I thought about my past relationship I would focus on the positive times, which in fact far outweighed the bad times (I changed the shade of my glasses). I changed my language so instead of saying 'my marriage *failed*' (failed implies that someone did something wrong), I started to say that 'the relationship *ended*', which is much more matter of fact and refrains from associating blame with any one party. In retrospect I don't believe anyone failed: we simply reached a point in our lives where it was no longer the right thing for us to be together.

The best part of this switch in my mindset happened when I identified what I had learned from the experience and recognized some of the less-empowering behaviours I had exhibited in response to some pretty intense stimuli. I was able to finally recognize my responsibility for the situation and I was no longer a victim of circumstances. I still didn't necessarily understand why everything that had happened happened, but now I had regained my power to choose the meaning that I associated with those events. Finally I was able to move on.

Now I'm unbelievably grateful for this past experience as I've learnt so much and it gave me an opportunity to make difference choices. As a result I now have the most amazing relationship which I share with my present husband. I know we wouldn't have the relationship we have now if I hadn't had this prior experience. I could have chosen to stay wounded and remain in pain even if I had buried those feelings deep into my unconscious. Yet that negativity would have slowly eaten away from the inside out and inevitably would have remanifested itself at some point, poisoning any future relationships. The only way to move on is to be able to release the past with joy by choosing to forgive.

"Forgiveness is not an occasional act, it is a permanent attitude."

Martin Luther King Jr., American civil rights leader and minister

How hot does it have to be, before you'll get out of the kitchen?

Have you ever wondered why some people leave one relationship then repeat the same pattern over and over again with all their future partners? They have the same relationship again and again, only with different people. They are still wearing the same shade of sunglasses and unconsciously continue to apply the past negative filters from their past experiences, which over time create the same current reality again and again.

Some people do this in their professional lives. When they become dissatisfied in their job then instead of dealing with the situation and their responsibility to it, they leave, start a new job and six months later find themselves in a different situation but dealing with the same stuff. Others do it in their finances: time goes by yet their circumstances never change, no matter how much money they earn, as they continue to repeat the same patterns in their money management. Some people do it with their bodies; they lose weight only to put it all back within a few months.

If you are living any negative, repetitive life experiences then I suggest you change your filters by healing your past. The most powerful way to heal is to decide to be grateful for the experience and focus on what you are able to learn from it, then apply the new meaning in your current reality.

Now that may appear to be easier said than done, particularly if the original stimulus that created your behaviour in the first place was particularly painful and may have been sustained over a long period of time. That builds up a huge amount of pain and suffering in your being. However, just decide to be grateful – it is that simple. You may have to do it more than once – every time you find yourself slipping back into your old negative ways of thinking – but each time a memory pops up in your mind, decide to choose to be grateful for that experience, since without it you wouldn't now possess the wisdom you have.

Look back at your original list from Chapter 1 where you recorded all the areas of your life that were causing you stress and pain. Take a moment to decide what you are able to draw from those memories – how they will serve and empower you now and into the future.

Examples of finding gratitude

- **A bad relationship**. You could decide to be grateful as it helped you understand the power of your own self-worth, and means that you now teach people how to respect you. Now you have more self-worth you are able to recognize that you can only be a victim if you *choose* to be a victim.
- **Struggling with debt**. You could decide to be grateful, for the experience has taught you the value of money. Now you appreciate

the lighter things in life that actually make you happy, and know that owning stuff is not worth the emotional trade-off of acquiring debt.

- **Bullied at work**. You could decide to be grateful as being exposed to that kind of behaviour has given you the wisdom to know how *not* to treat people.
- **Devastating illness**. You could decide to be grateful as you no longer take your health and physical body for granted. You realize you have the power to make changes in your lifestyle and choices, both at a physical and emotional level, as well as living in the now.
- **High-maintenance family unit**. You could decide to be grateful as your family relationships give you the opportunity to learn humility, respect, *patience*, love (in all its forms) and gratitude, as no other people act as a greater reflection back to you than your immediate family members.
- **Loss of love**. You could decide to be grateful for having had the experience of being loved. Even if you may think you've never been loved in your life, at some point everyone has been loved. A baby will lose weight and die of malnutrition (what the experts call 'failure to thrive' syndrome) if they are not caressed or spoken to and do not create a loving bond with someone. Regardless of whether their basic nutritional needs have been met, the baby will still die. Therefore, even if you have no conscious memory of ever having the experience of being loved, the fact that you are alive today, reading this, means that at some point in your life somebody, somewhere loved you.

"Everything can be taken away from man but one thing – to choose one's attitude in a given set of circumstances, to choose one's own way."

Viktor Frankl, psychiatrist and holocaust survivor

Repetition is the mother of all learning

So does this mean that once you've decide to forgive and move on that everything will change from that instant on? Sometimes – but it's much more likely that it will be a process and some days it will feel like two steps forward and one step back. That's OK, providing you are still moving forward.

There will be times and moments that you still find yourself being whacked over the head with a double whammy from the universe – the stimulus is so strong that you may find yourself being pulled off-centre. I can remember a moment 18 months after my divorce when I thought intellectually that I had long healed from the pain. I was in my car when a particular song came on the radio and it acted as a powerful trigger for all the past negative memories. I instantly turned into a gibbering wreck and had to pull over as I couldn't see through the tears to continue driving. However, I allowed myself that moment to mourn the loss of what could have been, but then once the song had finished I switched my thinking, instantly, to what I was grateful for and what I had learned from that part of my life. Within a few moments the pain passed and I was again empowered by my own possibility.

Providing you recognize when this happens and don't remain there indefinitely, then don't panic. It doesn't mean all your hard work up until now has been undone, simply that you've been 'whacked' by the universe's baseball bat.

The more you practise your new mindset, keep applying your new sunglasses, keep reassociating new meaning to negative events, the easier it becomes. Then one day it all clicks, you achieve full alignment and balance, and it simply becomes who you are, the type of person you are naturally – the New You has emerged.

It takes around 32 days of consistent application for a new mindset and behaviour to become habitual. Once you reach that stage, you will act in the new ways without even thinking about it. But just like when you first learn to drive a car, initially clunking the gears and bumping the kerb, you will find that to start with it may take a bit of effort. Don't beat yourself up if you catch yourself out. Just remember to consciously make the choice to feel and behave differently in the moment.

Repetition is the mother of all learning and eventually the New You will become stronger than the older version – so stick with it.

SUMMARY

- What you choose to perceive becomes your reality and how you experience life.

- Our brains filter our thoughts by generalizing, distorting or deleting incoming information based upon our past experiences.

- The more intense the emotion associated with a past experience, the more likely we are to recall it and use it to filter our current reality.

- You can choose whether to be a Tigger or an Eeyore.

- Change the meaning of your past by releasing all negativity: instead decide to be grateful and learn from the experience.

- Repetition is required to develop and condition new ways of thinking and develop new habits.

05

Yeah but, no but –
the power of reclaiming your
internal dialogue

Everybody has a little voice inside their head. In fact we usually have two: a positive, supportive voice and a 'yeah but, no but' negative voice. Whenever you are about to challenge yourself, say for example you need to make a speech in public, as if by magic, the voices appear. I call the negative version the 'Vicky Pollard' voice as a reference to the character in the British TV show *Little Britain*, made famous by Matt Lucas, where the character Vicky Pollard begins every sentence with a long garbled string of excuses starting 'Yeah but, no but, yeah but, no but'.

How you tackle any task in hand is linked directly to which voice you listen to, and more often than not the 'yeah but, no but' voice is much much louder. That unfortunately is often the reason we allow ourselves to be held back. Simply because a small voice inside is telling you,

'No don't try that – what if you make a fool of yourself?', or perhaps 'You're not worth it, so don't even bother trying', or even 'You're going to fail', or worse still, if it's a negative reflection of a current situation, 'See, you deserved that!'

Not many people naturally have an empowering voice which instead tells them things like 'Go on, you can do it', or 'Take the chance it may just work out', or even more powerfully 'You are able to achieve absolutely anything you set your mind and your heart to' – or, in the words of the L'Oréal adverts, 'You're worth it!'

The power of these voices is huge. Some people refer to them as your *self-talk* or your *internal dialogue*. Sigmund Freud, the grandfather of what we understand today to be the field of psychology, identified that the functions of the mind are split into three areas, one of them being what he referred to as *das Über-Ich* or, translated, the *super-ego*.

The term *super-ego* is used to describe the part of our personality which is mainly unconscious but includes our conscience reasoning, our ego, our goals and the part of us that criticizes and prohibits us. Anyone who has a negatively programmed super-ego will have poor self-esteem, low morale and very little confidence. They are unlikely to take risks in their lives and to ever try any new experiences unless it's a requirement or they are forced to do so.

People who have either a naturally empowering super-ego or have reprogrammed it, as you will learn how to, are the kind who are 'up for anything', seemingly fearless with bags of confidence. Sky diving with no parachutes: 'Count me in' they'd cry! (By the way, it is possible to do exactly that, jump out of an aeroplane with no parachute – you just have to hope that the person behind catches up with you before the ground does! Not that I've tried it, or indeed recommend it! I do however, recommend doing anything that you find personally challenging; it's what creates personal growth.)

This type of person is much more likely to live a life full of fun, enjoy new experiences, live with passion and joy, all due to their increased levels of confidence – and ultimately a much higher level of personal success. They step into the unknown often armed only with a strong self-belief.

Our reactions to our own super-ego trigger a very basic instinct within us where we choose either to take up the challenge or to flee the situation. So think about what your natural response is when you are challenged. Even though there may still be a part of you that turns to jelly, how do you naturally behave? Do you find every excuse in the book to fly from the challenge or do you stand firm?

This response, known as *fight or flight*, was first identified by American physiologist Walter Cannon in 1915, and is a physiological response in our bodies to imminent danger. It's designed to keep us alive, but just like many of the other functions of our mind, if it is left unchecked it can hinder and hold us back from fulfilling our true potential.

Should I stay or should I go?

One of the first parts of the human brain to form was the part at the back of the skull known as the reptilian brain, or to give it its proper name the R-complex, which includes the brain stem and the cerebellum. This part of our brain is working instinctively. It does not have the ability to reason or make logical or even emotional evaluations; its only job is to keep us alive. So should you ever find yourself in a life-threatening situation, the reptilian part of the brain kicks in and decides in a split second whether you should stay and defend yourself or run as fast as you can to get away. Either way it floods your body with adrenalin to prepare your muscles to take the necessary action.

As with many ways in which our brains are hard-wired, this brain function worked brilliantly for us when we were living in much more primitive environments where we were under threat from predators. You wouldn't want to spend time evaluating a situation when a big, hungry, grizzly bear is heading your way. You want to be out of there as quickly as you possibly can.

However, in modern day life in most civilized cultures our lives are not under threat from hostile environments in the same way, so we do not need to react using our instinctive stress response. Yet biologically, when we allow the negative Vicky Pollard voice to overpower our decisions, that is what we're doing. We are allowing our survival instinct to drive our behaviour.

From a health perspective the long-term impact of continued fight or flight or stress responses, particularly when triggered in situations that do not require physical exertion, are huge. In the moment when the stress response is triggered the body shuts down the digestive system as well as our sex drive and any other non-critical bodily function to allow us to focus on the immediate danger. However, if this is sustained over a period of time, it can result in, amongst other things, diarrhoea, constipation, low libido, suppression of the immune system – all ultimately leading to an imbalance which eventually leads to disease manifesting somewhere down the line. If we learn to control our negative internal dialogue and eliminate the 'yeah but, no but' elements from our lives, not only will we increase our levels of confidence and create more success, but will remain healthier as well.

The World Health Organization has calculated that a person with sustained mental health disorder (of which depression is the most common) will reduce their life expectancy by an average of 12 years. All the more reason to learn how to manage that stress response and improve your overall mental health.

So suppose you're offered an opportunity at work that will require you to try something new and for which you have no past experience to draw on. When your Vicky Pollard voice chirps up with 'Say no – you can't do it', remember it's simply your fight or flight response trying to protect you from what it perceives to be imminent danger, when in real terms it quite clearly isn't.

HOW DO YOU BEGIN TO CHANGE YOUR NATURAL INSTINCTIVE RESPONSE?

If you're not naturally the type of person who would take a risk or you feel that you are holding yourself back in a particular area of your life, how do you begin to change your natural instinctive response?

Feel the fear and do it anyway

Feel the Fear and Do It Anyway is an awesome book written by the psychotherapist and counsellor Dr Susan Jeffers, and as the title suggests it is all about stretching beyond your comfort zone.

Around us all we have a self-imposed comfort zone, created as a result of the self-imposed limitations of our super-ego, guided by our fight or flight responses. Whilst we behave within that comfort zone and our actions or choices never require us to do anything new or different, then that's fine, because everything feels *comfortable.*

Some people's comfort zones are much bigger than others due to the experiences and choices they've made, but everyone has one. Often we have different comfort zones for different areas of our lives. We may feel extremely confident in our job because we have been well trained and we have lots of experience, but when it comes to relationships that confidence abandons us. Perhaps you have lots of body confidence and work hard to stay in shape, yet if you're asked to step up in public and make a speech, suddenly you become highly self-conscious, your knees turn to jelly and you fluff your words.

When this happens and your body responds like this or in similar ways, it is simply an indication that you have stepped beyond your comfort zone and you have now entered the scary world of the unknown.

Some people are better at dealing with this than others because they have a more empowering version of the Vicky Pollard voice.

Life will always require us to break beyond the confines of our comfort zones over and over again; from the first time you went swimming without armbands, to your first day at school, to the first day in a new job or when you received a promotion. The first time you went on a date, your first driving lesson, all of these are examples of moving beyond your comfort zone.

As you go through life you move outside your comfort zone either because you are *required* to or because you *choose* to, and those who choose to are the people who also have the greatest levels of confidence and ultimately the greatest levels of personal success. Therefore, in order to gain more confidence you need to learn how to overpower this internal voice when it's holding you back. The way to do this is by using mantras.

Fear vs. instinct

Managing your fear and your body's natural stress response, which left unchecked can accumulate stress in your system, is very different from listening to your natural instincts, which if you find yourself in a potentially dangerous situation, are designed to keep you alive and out of danger. You should always listen to instinct, but be aware of the difference between instinct and fear.

So if you find yourself about to enter a lift, for example, and every instinct in your body is telling you something isn't right and you feel threatened by the only other person also about to enter the lift, *then take the stairs*. Don't put yourself in unnecessary possible danger. This is an example of when you *should* listen to your body's instincts. On the other hand, if you are offered a chance to do something new and potentially life enhancing, but have a little voice telling you that you can't do it – that's when you need to override the voice.

We are the only animals on the planet who ignore our instincts when we really should be listening to them, yet allow our false fears to rampage unchecked through our lives, allowing them to keep us within our comfort zones and stopping us from achieving our true potential. Your job is to learn to make the distinction between the two situations.

Develop your personal mantra

A mantra is a phrase or a statement of intention which by constant repetition drowns out any negative internal dialogue and also has the added bonus of building self-belief.

I have used mantras for many years now and believe them to be fundamentally responsible for the positive changes I've made. They are the one technique I draw on whenever I'm feeling in need of a confidence boost.

Mantras are different from power questions, which are designed to change the meaning or reframe a situation. Mantras are designed to increase your confidence and propel you into action, but they work in a similar way to power questions.

When designing your mantra there are four simple rules you must apply.

1 Make it positive

This may seem pretty obvious: if the purpose is to overpower the negative Vicky Pollard voice in your head the last thing you want to do is give even more power to the 'no buts'! However, many people don't realize the emotional intensity behind the words they use and the power they have.

I personally believe in the power of words so strongly that I would never wear a T-shirt if it had negative words in a slogan. I won't even allow my young son to wear T-shirts that proudly state 'I'm a little monster' or 'Here comes trouble' – they may be cute but I simply don't want him exposed to messages like this. Words can have a very great influence on what people become, so a child given the message he is trouble is more likely to become trouble.

This is also why, as I mentioned earlier, I changed my language about the end of my first marriage: I purposefully stopped using the word 'failed'.

When you create a mantra for yourself, avoid using what I call *moving away from* language to describe what you don't want. Instead choose a mantra to state what you absolutely do intend.

MANY PEOPLE DON'T REALIZE THE EMOTIONAL INTENSITY BEHIND THE WORDS THEY USE.

So, for example, 'I no longer feel stressed' would still have a negative effect as the negative implication of the word 'stressed' would still bring the effects of stress higher into your consciousness. A better example would be 'I am feeling calm and balanced'. Always choose positive empowering language.

2 State it in the present tense

Using a mantra that is future based means the results will always be future based. 'I will achieve my goals' is less powerful than 'I am achieving my goals – *now!*' When you pronounce your intentions as if they have already happened, that kick-starts your consciousness to make it happen now.

The deeper unconscious parts of our brains hate disorder. So, for example, if current circumstances are different from your beliefs, which have been created by repeating your mantra over and over again, you activate a deep-rooted part of your higher consciousness to get on with matters to, in the words of the famous Captain Kirk, 'make it so'.

One of the strongest needs within our personality, as described by Freud in his work with the id, ego and super-ego, is the need to match what our ego perceives with reality. This explains why our brains require order, or at least for things to match with how we perceive them. This also explains why we apply filters in our lives, to 'trick' ourselves into believing what our internal drivers perceive to already be true.

Therefore, if we create a mantra that is different from our current circumstances, the more powerful it becomes by constant repetition, the faster our mind works and drives us to match our current situation with our internal programming.

So, for example, you might say 'I have all the confidence I need within me now' (which by the way is one of my favourite personal mantras). Then even if at the time you initially say it you actually don't feel confident – perhaps you're about to make that speech we mentioned earlier – your mind wakes up with a lightning flash and asks 'Oh OK, in order for this to be true, what do we need to do to feel confident?' Then your brain will release the necessary hormones to *enable* you to feel the confidence you desire.

3 Make it about you personally

The purpose of a mantra is to change your emotions and behaviour, not someone else's. So there is no point at all creating a mantra such as 'They need to be more loving' or 'They need to understand me'. Oh no, no, no. All you do when you think like this is once again redirect your focus outwards to an external stimulus that is beyond your control. You actually give away your power. Remember the only choice you *ever* have is how you choose to behave in response to the things that happen to you.

When a pebble is thrown into a pond it causes a series of ripples to radiate outwards from the point of entry. Create a mantra that is directed towards your own behaviour and you are the pebble; create a mantra directed towards someone else's behaviour and you are the ripples, helpless against the changes that happen around you.

So make sure your mantras are about you and what you need to change.

4 Say it out loud and say it proud!

The final element to make a mantra truly powerful is to say it *out loud*! When you give life to words, by proclaiming them out loud you intensify the emotions behind the statement – and remember how crucial emotions are. Ultimately you are your emotions. They drive your behaviour, which in turn leads to your outcomes. The more emotional intensity behind an experience, the more we draw upon it to filter our current reality and the more likely you are to drown out the negative Vicky Pollard voice.

When you speak you also move your body, which again amplifies the impact of what you say. The more powerful your body language the more intensified the emotional response. Anyone who has ever seen the All Blacks, the New Zealand rugby team, perform their 'Haka' at the beginning of a game, can appreciate the power of speaking out loud and moving your body as well as stating your mantra. Obviously the Haka originated as a war dance, but the All Blacks use it as a way of ensuring the team is pumped up before the game begins. Anyone who has ever witnessed the Haka first hand would agree that the team becomes *extremely* pumped up and in fighting spirit.

Now that doesn't mean you have to perform a war dance before you do anything. This depends on what your desired outcome is, but it is important that you say your mantra out loud. So pick a time and place that is appropriate to you, perhaps in the shower or in the car on your way to a sales meeting, and say your mantra three to five times out loud, expressing the emotional state you wish to recreate with as much emotional intensity as you can muster.

A mantra for every occasion

You can create as many mantras as you wish. Design them for every area of your life then use them regularly. Make stating your mantras a part of your daily routine, as regular as cleaning your teeth. Think of them as 'cleaning your mind of the negativity' – just like cleaning your teeth every morning and evening removes the plaque that builds up overnight.

Use mantras in the moments when you feel vulnerable to your negative Vicky Pollard voice, but for the next 32 days use a mantra that works on one of the key areas of your life that you need to regain some power over, and say it three to five times out loud, three times a day. Each time you say it, change your tone and emphasise different words in the mantra as this also builds even more belief. Remember to move your body in a way that represents the way you want to feel, or feel more of.

So, for example, 'All I *need* is within me now', followed by '*All* I need is within me now', followed again by 'All I need is within *me* now', and so on.

More ideas to get you started

- I am courageous and bold.
- I am living my best life.
- I am stronger than the negative events that happen to me.
- My purpose is to live and to love, even when I do not understand.
- Strength is in me and all around me.
- Abundance is everywhere and I am part of it.
- I believe in my power of what is possible.
- I choose my life and it's awesome!

"I believe anyone can conquer fear by doing the things he fears to do, provided he keeps on doing them until he gets a record of successful experiences behind him."

Eleanor Roosevelt, First Lady of the United States

SUMMARY

- Everyone has a positive and a negative super-ego, or as I call it the Vicky Pollard voice – 'yeah but, no but'.

- The reptilian brain within us reacts to what it perceives to be imminent danger by activating our stress response: *fight or flight*.

- In order to increase your confidence you need to get outside your comfort zone more often.

- Develop mantras as a way to recondition your super-ego by following four simple rules:

  1 Use positive language.

  2 State them in the present tense.

  3 They must be about you.

  4 *Say them out loud*!

06

Believe and succeed –
the power of unending belief

Nothing happens in life before we believe it will happen. Ultimately you create the levels of success you want in your life based upon your belief. The belief that you are capable of the most fulfilling intimate relationship, the most amazing business success, the most energetic levels of vitality, the highest levels of financial freedom, the most balanced happy children, in fact whatever you desire, is a result of faith.

Through your thoughts, feelings and behaviours you draw to you the results and success you desire. Often when things are not going your way and the going gets tough in your life, a beloved friend will suggest you 'have faith'. So what do they mean?

What is faith?

We can describe *faith* as the trust in future outcomes or life experiences, long before they are proven to be true.

I remember going through a pretty scary moment in my business when three or four negative things all happened in very quick succession. A couple of new contracts we were expecting were all postponed six months or more, a major client defaulted on their payment, and boom – suddenly our cash flow was negative and with very little confirmed new business in the order book, my faith deserted me!

Suddenly life became very hard. I had gone from being in the flow to suddenly swimming upstream like a swan – all serene and beautiful on the outside but my feet paddling away like mad underneath! I was tired and feeling overwhelmed and then one particular day when I felt pretty close to wanting to hide under the duvet for good, I reminded myself that I needed to rediscover my faith. I needed to look forward, not wallow in the current negative situation, particularly regarding things that I couldn't directly change.

So I picked myself up and took action. I sat down with my team and on a practical level we made some instant cost-cutting decisions. We gave notice on our premises and found a cheaper alternative. We devised a new strategy which we all felt positive about and, most importantly, together we all focused on our uniqueness with absolute faith that everything would soon turn positive. However, the major change we all made individually was to twice a day visualize the positive changes we believed would happen, happening now. Almost instantly we landed some major new business and in fact our business started to grow and consequently our cash flow improved quite dramatically.

"The secret of making something work in your lives is first of all, the deep desire to make it work; then the faith and belief that it can work; then to hold that clear definite vision in your consciousness and see it working out step by step, without one thought of doubt or disbelief."

Eileen Caddy, co-founder of the Findforn Foundation

The life you are currently living is a product of your past thinking, just as the future you create is based on what you believe now, and what you believe to be possible. When a pebble is thrown into the middle of a pond, the ripples do not appear simultaneously, they radiate out from the centre. Your belief works in just the same way. The thoughts you have today do not instantly come true, sometimes you need to hang on to your faith for quite some time before you begin to see the changes in your life and the ripple you're waiting for is created.

Usually the biggest rewards take the longest time, effort and faith to achieve and on the journey you can expect to have setbacks;

that's when your faith in achieving your overall goal will be tested. It's almost as if this time the universe, instead of holding a baseball bat, has now turned into a saboteur – just when you can see the finish line, it chucks a load of obstacles in the way and some hot tar across

your path, and then ties your legs together – just to increase the stakes. All as if to say, 'Come on you, how much do you really want this? Are you up for the challenge or are you going to roll over and give up?' Those that choose to take up the challenge will not only personally grow as a consequence but *will* also achieve their goals. Those who choose the opposite will start perfecting their *victim* stories about the reasons why their success was denied them.

When I think back to that moment in my business when I really didn't know where the next penny would come from and I didn't know how I would be able to pay my team their wages at the end of the month, it made me question *everything*. Am I in the right market? Are we offering the right products and services? Are my team the right people? Should I even have a business at all!?

If everything had been going hunky dory and we had tons of cash in the bank I would *never* have had a shred of doubt. My faith was being truly tested.

In my heart I knew that although this particular experience was not pleasant, it would pass and that I, the team and the business would all grow as a result. I hung on to my faith. Meanwhile I was also inspired by the team and everyone around me, who also demonstrated solid faith – in me, in what we do, and how we do it. Everyone in the business just got to work visualizing the current situation turning around.

Religious faith is based on an agreed set of principles, which are different for each school of thought but are all based on the theology of a 'supreme' being or something bigger than us, guiding us and connecting us to a higher source. So whether you have faith in a religious set of principles or not, whether you believe you are being guided by a higher force or not, in order to create the levels of success you desire, you absolutely *must* have belief in your own power and your own potential. Without that, without the *power of possibility*, you will never achieve your full potential and therefore never live your best life.

Those who believe they can, will. They use their Scooby ears to work out whether they are getting closer or further away from where they would like to be, before applying the principles of behavioural flexibility to change their approach until they eventually achieve their goals, no matter how difficult or how many times they have to change. Others won't. Instead they focus on everything that is going wrong, they don't have any faith that things could be different now or ever, which only per-petuates the cycle of negativity in their future.

YOU ABSOLUTELY MUST HAVE BELIEF IN YOUR OWN POWER AND YOUR OWN POTENTIAL.

Create your vision

To create belief in yourself you first need to experience the outcome – *before* it has been created – and you do this through creating your *vision*. A vision is much more than just deciding what you want, although this is a necessary step. The process of creative visualization allows you to experience fully at an emotional level how achieving your goals feels. This gives your mind, at an unconscious level, more focus, creativity, motivation and drive to do whatever it takes to achieve your goals. Some even believe that it draws your goals closer to you even faster, through one of the laws of the universe known as the 'law of attraction', which is based on the principle that like attracts like.

The process of visualization has long been recognized as a powerful tool that has been proven to increase the incidence of the event or circumstances becoming true.

The Disney dream

At the opening ceremony of the Walt Disney World Resort in Florida in October 1967, one year after the death of Walt, a journalist famously stated to Lillian, Walt's wife, 'Isn't it a shame Walt isn't here to see the dream become reality', to which Lillian wisely replied, 'The reason you're here seeing it and experiencing it, is because Walt saw it'. Walt Disney had the vision long before the reality came true. He visualized the concept and the detail, so no matter how long and arduous the journey took he kept his eye on the horizon and firmly believed in his dream becoming reality. Even though he did not live to see the dream become actuality, it did not matter: he had already experienced it – in his imagination.

I do not know of anyone who has achieved anything remarkable in their life without creating a vision and having faith that they will get there.

When you visualize in your mind you do more than just create a picture, you create a pattern of brain waves as if you had actually executed and achieved your desired outcome. The more your reassociate with your vision and your dreams, the more you create belief. This has become common practice in sports psychology, with all the top athletes in the world placing as much emphasis on visualizing their victories to create faith and positive belief as on training physically. They need to be in the best physical *and* mental condition to win.

The 4-minute mile

Timed foot races by men were first recorded from the 1850s, and in 1886 Walker George set what at the time everyone believed to be an unbeatable record of 4.12 seconds for a mile run. Over the next 50 years the ambition for a human man to run a 4-minute mile became an obsession with numerous athletes who attempted and failed to break through the perceived impossible barrier.

Roger Bannister became the first man ever to do so on 6 May 1954 at Oxford University. However, after only 46 days Australian John Landy equalled the record. Over the latter part of the twentieth century 17 more seconds were shaved off the record and today the 4-minute mile has become the benchmark by which all amateur athletes are measured.

So why did the record stand unbeaten for 60 years only to be broken twice in 46 days? Simply because it was widely accepted, until Roger Bannister proved everyone wrong, that it was physically impossible for a man to run a mile in under 4 minutes. After that *everyone's* belief changed, but Roger had had the strongest belief of anyone – not only that it could be done but that he would be the first man in the world to do so. That's why his legacy can never be taken away from him.

It's also widely reported that many highly successful individuals actively created visons to build belief and move them faster to their goals. People like Jim Carrey, Oprah Winfrey, Richard Branson and Bill Gates all spend a few moments a couple of times a day to focus on their dreams, imagining them all being true.

Remember your present circumstances are merely the manifestations, through your actions, behaviours and choices, of your past thinking. Therefore, in order to change your future you must focus on its possibilities and live in a way as if they are already reality.

Most people fail because they give up just before the moment of breakthrough, just as they are about to achieve the success they want. Success does not discriminate – it simply rewards those that keep on believing. The stronger your belief, the faster it will happen.

Get into the 'alpha zone'

Your brain activity works on four levels: beta, alpha, theta and delta, depending on how fast you think. *Beta* brain vibrations are most dominant in your normal waking state and are most prevalent when you talk and move. *Alpha* brain waves work at a slighter slower pace and are activated when you are more relaxed and allow your unconscious mind to come to the fore.

Theta activity occurs when you drift off into a light sleep. This is the time when REM (rapid eye movement) sleep occurs and you dream, which is your brain's way of organizing information and solving problems. That's why you can wake up from a deep sleep because you've remembered someone's name when it had eluded you earlier in the day. Your brain is so excited that it found the information, it must wake you up immediately to let you know! Even if you do not remember your dreams, studies have shown that everyone dreams at some point throughout the night.

Finally, *delta* brain activity only occurs in the deepest form of sleep. It allows our bodies to rejuvenate and repair and only in this state do our brains release human growth hormone, which is the stuff that keeps us young! This explains why babies and toddlers sleep so much – it's when they get on with the important job of growing! It is also why when we are ill we naturally want to sleep, as our bodies require us to shut down in order to get on with the job of healing. When you've not had enough sleep you look and feel old when you wake up.

So, for example, when you first learn to drive a car, your brain will be running at beta levels, but if you are an experienced driver, driving often feels like you are on 'auto-pilot'. You may even arrive at your destination and have no conscious memory of your journey – instead you have been daydreaming, mentally planning your day or going over a problem in your head. These are all examples of your brain working in the alpha zone. We can induce the alpha state by practising relaxation, meditation and visualization techniques. I was very good at getting into my alpha zone at school – forever being told off for daydreaming while looking out of the window instead of paying attention in class!

The technique of visualization occurs when you are in a meditative state, and your brain activity is activated at the alpha levels of vibration, so in order to create your vision you need to become a master of relaxation.

In our daily lives we are always so busy, so it's unlikely, unless you consciously build it into your daily routine, that you would

IN ORDER TO CREATE YOUR VISION YOU NEED TO BECOME A MASTER OF RELAXATION.

naturally choose to create your future through the power of visualization. We live our lives at beta busyness, then drop into theta sleep brain waves, physically and emotionally exhausted.

Learning to hold your brain in the alpha zone does take a bit of practice. If you're not used to practising relaxation it's common to drop off to sleep, as the moment you close your eyes your brain goes, 'Oh, OK so we're going to sleep now, are we?' So here are some tips to get you started.

Practising relaxation – getting into the alpha zone

- Choose a time of day when you are able to have 20 minutes of uninterrupted 'me' time. Perhaps first thing in the morning, or in the sauna after a workout at the gym, whilst lying in a nice warm bath or in a quiet moment during your working day. If you haven't got a spare 20 minutes, make time. This is a crucial part of you achieving your full potential, so rearrange your schedule, or ask someone to watch the kids – just make sure you do it.

- Turn off your phone and make sure you are not going to be interrupted.

- Make yourself comfortable, but if you're new to this I would suggest sitting comfortably as opposed to lying down on your bed, as your brain will associate that behaviour with going to sleep. Instead find a comfortable chair and place both your feet on the floor with your arms loosely relaxed by your sides.

- Drink a nice big glass of water before you begin.

- If it helps, play some soothing music in the background, or, as my husband calls it, 'plinky-plonk' music. There are plenty of CDs out there to choose from, everything from 'whale music' to 'angel music'. Choose music that you like, but which doesn't have any lyrics or an upbeat rhythm, as these will only bring your brain back up to beta activity.

- Close your eyes and focus on your breathing for around 10 breaths. You will probably find that thoughts pop in and out of your brain. You may be 'off shopping' for a moment or two but that's OK – allow your thoughts to flow freely, without holding on to any of them.

- Then choose a goal or an outcome you want to achieve. This could be a long-term goal that you envisage some time further in the future, or it could be simply what you want to achieve that day, or even in the next conversation you intend to have. In your imagination see yourself achieving your outcome; take a few moments to live it. What does it look like, sound like, smell like, taste like and, most importantly, how does it feel? What emotions are you feeling when you see yourself achieving your outcome?

- With your next deep breath in, step fully into the image, if you are not there already, by seeing it through your own eyes as opposed to observing yourself in the image.

- Stay in the moment as long as you choose to and fully associate with the pleasurable images, sounds and emotions you are experiencing. Remember the more emotional intensity we attach to the events that occur (even the ones we create in our mind), the more powerful the motivators in our brain.

- When you're ready to return to full consciousness, become aware once again of your breathing. Wiggle your fingers and toes before opening your eyes and giving your body a nice stretch.

If you are new to this, and are finding it difficult to get into the zone, then perhaps it may help to use a 'guided visualization' CD to get you started. As well as the relaxing music a narrator will give your conscious brain a series of suggestions to help your imagination fill in the blanks. To download our version visit www.auroratraining.com

Alternatively you could go all out and book yourself on to a meditation retreat or at least a session in a flotation tank, both of which will help you develop your meditation techniques. Just like you would work out your physical body in the gym to keep it in tip-top condition, learn how to become a master of visualizations and condition your mind to achieve. That is where your belief and ultimately your faith comes from.

If you've ever rehearsed an argument with your partner before you get home, or planned an event in your mind, maybe a family Christmas for example, you are already using visualization. Yet normally we mentally rehearse all the negative and stressful things in our lives, so instead decide to use visualization to focus on your goals and what you want out of life, even if you do not yet know *how* you will achieve them. That's the fun part of your life experience – working out how to make your dreams come true.

The more your psyche believes you have already achieved your goals, the more your focus will uncover the methods you need to use to reach them.

Jack Canfield, the author of *Chicken Soup for the Soul*, recounts a fabulous metaphor that demonstrates this point. If you are driving in the dark, your car headlights only ever allow you to see 20 yards in front of you, yet because you know your end goal, where you ultimately want to get to, you continue to steadily move forward on your journey, trusting that the next 20 yards will be revealed until you reach your destination.

"Never look down to test the ground before taking the next step; only he who keeps his eye fixed on the far horizon will find his right road."

Dag Hammarskjöld, Secretary General of the UN

Turn your problems into problems solved

When you feel you have a problem and that you're stuck with no alternatives, you block your creative thinking which would help you find ways of overcoming the problem. So if you currently feel 'stuck' in a particular area of your life, use your new-found visualization techniques to find creative ways to overcome the problem.

If you are about to take on a big challenge or move your life in a new direction then you can also anticipate the problems before they occur and in your creative visualization see yourself overcoming them.

Deborah Veal is a remarkable young woman – she rowed the Atlantic solo in 2001. She did not intend to row the Atlantic solo but when her rowing partner had to be rescued early into their journey everyone expected Deborah to give up. However Deborah had visualized achieving her end goal to such a profound extent, in her mind there was no alternative other than to carry on and cross the finish line.

The journey that should have taken six weeks instead took Deborah three and a half gruelling months. When she had been preparing for her journey, before she even knew she would be completing the journey alone, she would run through in her mind every possible outcome, every little thing that could go wrong and visualize being able to solve it. So, for example, she practised in her mind fixing the water pump, then fixing the water pump in a gale, then fixing the water pump in a gale in the middle of the night! So when she actually found herself in that exact situation – fixing the water pump in a gale in the middle of the night – she had no fear. She had already practised, albeit in her mind, solving the problem. So instead she simply executed her plan and got on with it – problem solved.

So creative visualization can also be used to pre-empt and then solve problems too. Ultimately all you want to achieve is that positive outcome.

Here are some examples of typical blips that can occur in otherwise seemingly positive circumstances that you can practise handling and overcoming. Then if they do happen for real, you don't freak out; you simply execute your plan and get on and deal with them:

- a dissatisfied client situation being resolved
- a poorly family member, or even yourself, recovering from illness
- a disconnected intimate relationship reconnecting
- a quarrel with a friend being put to rest
- a child's tantrum passing
- a financial struggle being replaced with wealth and abundance.

I used this technique to massive effect when I was preparing for the labour and birth of my son. I had every anticipation that it would be painful – I've seen plenty of TV births and it didn't look like a picnic to me. Plus my bump was scarily huge!

So every evening for 10 weeks leading up to the birth I visualized the whole labour process for around 20–30 minutes each night. In my visualization I acknowledged that I would be in pain but I saw myself having faith in my body's ability to bring my child into the world in a relaxed, calm and nurturing way, whilst being 'on top' of the pain. Every time I visualized the birth I played a particular piece of music to allow my brain to associate the deep feelings of relaxation with that particular piece.

When I did actually go into labour I found it to be one of the most empowering experiences of my life and happened almost exactly how I'd 'practised' it in my mind. I played the relaxing music that reminded my brain of the calming relaxed state I had previously entered. I was aware on some level that I was in pain, but I was so deeply relaxed, I was simply replaying the 'film' I had already created in my mind and, as a result, I was able to deal with the sensations in the most empowering way possible.

I did not need any medical intervention and was able to enjoy a very natural and amazingly enjoyable experience to welcome my son into the world. Afterwards the midwife commented that she hadn't seen many women be able to get 'into their zone' and be so relaxed throughout labour.

Although some people would say that I was simply 'lucky', I truly believe that my previous work at creatively visualizing the best possible outcome, through what can potentially be a very scary experience, empowered me to have faith in my body's ability to do what it needed to do.

You can use the same technique for any area in your life. Creating business success, developing amazing relationships, possessing the best health possible – it all happens because you first believe it can, and you have faith in your own power to create it. Your success is limitless – you and everyone you know is capable of absolutely anything, if you believe it to be true.

Remember success does not discriminate – it simply rewards those that keep on believing. The decision is yours.

SUMMARY

- Faith is ultimately the process of placing your trust in future outcomes.

- Success always follows faith in what you believe you can achieve.

- Create faith by using visualization as a method to emotionally experience your goals *before* they happen.

- Creative visualization is a skill which is practised when we are mentally relaxed.

- Use visualization not only to associate massively with goals, but also to solve problems in the most empowering way.

07

Define the New You –
the power of discovering
your true identity

Nature vs. nurture – the age-old debate. Are we a product of our predetermined DNA structure or are our personalities and our behaviours shaped by our environment and the experiences we've had?

Like many others, I firmly believe that nurture has a very dominant part to play in how we turn out. I believe very strongly that, although we have a genetic make-up that gives us the possibility to develop certain character traits, ultimately our identities are a product not only of the experiences we've had in life, but how *we've responded to those events and experiences* in our life thus far.

Everything that has happened to you so far in your life has left an imprint on you. Your early circumstances and the people whom you grew up around, your role models at school, the people you've worked with, the relationships you've shared – everyone and everything, particularly how you've learned to behave as a result, has had an impact on the kind of person you've become.

This is not negative, in fact it's very powerful. It means that if you feel there is a part of you that is destined to become more, that could be different, you have the power within you to change it! If you believe that we are only a product of our gene pool ('It's just the way I am') then it means you take no responsibility for yourself or your life experience. This other way means you have the power to change and reform anything about yourself. How awesome is that?

IT'S TIME TO STOP SITTING IN THE PASSENGER SEAT OF YOUR LIFE; INSTEAD TAKE CONTROL OF THE STEERING WHEEL.

Here are a couple of examples.

1 Healing a destructive family relationship

Here's an example from my own life that has had a profound impact on one of my most important relationships, the relationship with my mother. I love my mother dearly, but there was a time in my life (like most girls growing up) when all we ever seemed to do was argue. Our rows were legendary to the point that my Dad has been known to comment that two Rottweilers would communicate better. I seemed to be pre-programmed to instantly react to her. I was always on the defensive. Sometimes we didn't even have to speak – just being in the same room together would make my hackles rise and I was prepared to 'fight' at any moment.

Clearly this wasn't a healthy relationship, but this pattern of behaviour continued for many, many years – well past puberty and into adulthood. She would shout, I would shout back. She would accuse and I would defend, and of course nobody ever 'won' in these situations. Instead all we did was walk away feeling wounded and stockpile even more negative emotion as fuel for the next row, which was usually never too far away.

Intellectually we both knew that this behaviour wasn't healthy yet both of us were so caught up in blaming the other person that we were powerless to change it. Then one day I simply decided I wasn't going to argue with her anymore, it just became too important. So I used the 'eight steps to success' to stay in control of my own emotions and my responses to the circumstances. One of my power questions was to ask: 'I wonder what has happened today to make Mum feel so stressed?' Meanwhile one of my mantras was simply: 'I am always in control of my emotions and my behaviour and I choose to behave positively – right now!'

The situation between us didn't change instantly but I hung on to the belief that we would develop a lovingly warm relationship based on mutual respect. My dear Mum was obviously unaware of the reasons for the changes in my behaviour and was still expecting me to argue back! So when I refused to be drawn into the disagreements, very often she simply turned up the heat and tried her damnedest to make me argue back. Sometimes she really upped the stakes, which gave me *so* many opportunities to test my new found self-control. However, I continued to keep my cool, and I kept my cool some more and then some more – then finally the magic happened.

A whole *two years* after I had consciously taken this decision, she turned round to me. I remember the moment as if it was only yesterday. We were standing in the middle of her kitchen and she had been ranting on about something, I forget what, and she simply said, 'You're not going to argue with me, are you?!' I swear a choir singing the 'Hallelujah' chorus jumped out of the fridge! I was so pleased. Because I had continuously responded with positive behaviour to a negative situation – *eventually* it had created the positive reaction I had wanted. My changes led to empowering changes in someone else and in the overall situation.

"Be the change you want to see in the world."

Mahatma Gandhi, spiritual leader

Having said all of that, of course we are mother and daughter and we still have our moments, but I'm very pleased to say that our relationship today is vastly different from the relationship we shared 10 years ago.

2 Dealing with a complaint

Suppose a customer at work makes a complaint. Although your natural instinct might be to want to go on the offensive and defend yourself, your colleagues or your company, instead take a deep breath and ask what would be the best possible outcome from this situation.

A great power question to ask in this situation is: 'I wonder what this person's biggest driving emotion is, how they expected to fulfil that with our product or service, and I wonder where we fell short of their expectations?'

In order to control your frustration and negative emotions you could choose to reframe the situation into a positive one: this client's feedback will allow you to grow and become better at your job and as a company.

Next, before you respond to the client's complaint, it may be useful to power up with a positive mantra to ensure your behaviour empowers the situation. Here's a great example:

'I can deal positively with this situation and gain a perfect outcome for myself, the client and the business.'

By following the eight steps you are much more likely to respond positively and achieve a more positive outcome as opposed to allowing yourself to react unchecked to the potentially challenging stimulus.

The same kind of process works if a neighbour complains about something you or your family have done. Deep breath, ask yourself a power question about the person's driving emotion (is it control or envy, for example?). Reframe the situation to feel positive (the better you can get on with your neighbours, the better for a harmonious life – and at least now you know what's bothering them) and perform a quick run through of a suitable mantra to make sure you stay calm and handle the situation as positively as possible.

The power in a name

Is a name important? Absolutely, it defines your identity. You may love or hate your name; you may have several names –

either nicknames or even different last names: for example maiden name (professionally) and married name (for personal life). However many names you have, it's important you decide which name reflects your new improved identity, one that you can refer to when you need to reconnect with the New You – that's the name you need to find now.

I've had lots of name variations over the years. When I went through one of the biggest periods of personal transformation in my life, a good friend of mine, Michael Heppell, gave me a nickname. I don't know where it came from but it felt right and it stuck. It's not a name that many people know about and it's not a name you would hear me use outwardly on a daily basis, but it's the name I refer to privately that reminds me of my inner self, and my inner strength. So if I ever have a moment of self-doubt then I ask my nickname how she would handle the situation.

Everyone in my life has nicknames, but not ones I've come up with – I've asked them what name makes them feel most powerful and whether they would be happy for me to use it, especially if it empowers them. It's a great way to give yourself or someone else a boost but you must get it right. You know how irritating it is if someone refers to you by a derivative of your name – it can be extremely offensive. So make sure you ask before you start calling Daniel, Danny or Dan, or even Danno or Big D.

Your name is a reflection of your identity and nothing sounds sweeter to a person than the sound of their own name. So name

IS A NAME IMPORTANT? ABSOLUTELY, IT DEFINES YOUR IDENTITY.

the New You with a fond name that reflects your inner strength. It could be a nickname a beloved family member gave you when you were small or it could be one you decide now. So what's your real name?

Enjoy the journey

Now that you've mastered your mindset and you have the strength within you to maintain a powerful psychology, it's time to embark on the next stage in your journey to a New You by equipping yourself with a toolbox full of skills that will help you create the success you deserve.

It's worth remembering that life is not just a destination but a journey. Everyone experiences highs and lows and by using the techniques in this book you have the ability to reduce the lows and make the highs even higher. However, if you only place your focus in the future, you could be in danger of missing the joy and pleasurable experiences that are right under your nose every day.

The view from the top

A friend of mine accepted a challenge to climb and then stand on the top of a telegraph pole (under supervision and with a safety harness attached I might add!). His only focus was to achieve the target of successfully climbing the pole and standing on the top. In order to overcome his fear, he set off at an incredible rate of knots, flying up the pole without stopping. Of course he executed the exercise perfectly; only afterwards when he had returned to the ground did he comment to me that he had missed the opportunity to take in the views on the way up and even from the top!

If we're not careful we can miss the joy that is all around us every day, which creates a paradox. Should we focus on the horizon and the future we want to create, or should we live in the moment and be grateful for what we have now?

I believe a balanced life is a combination of both. Every day you should focus on your longer-term goals and gradually move in that direction, as well as each day finding time to appreciate the joy in the moment. That way you'll continue to achieve your dreams as well as enjoy the ride getting there.

If you don't find ways to achieve this balance and enjoy your life now, throwing all your hope and energy on to events in the future – 'Everything will be alright when we win the lottery', 'It'll all come good when I retire', 'I'll get my life back when the kids start school' and so on – means that when you get there you could be bitterly disappointed. You'll never achieve that feeling of inner peace and contentment, where you appreciate your life for what it is. Happiness is a feeling from within and you can choose to be happy right now whilst you continue to strive towards greater levels of personal success.

"One of the most tragic things I know about human nature is that all of us tend to put off living. We are all dreaming of some magical rose garden over the horizon instead of enjoying the roses that are blooming outside our windows today."

Dale Carnegie, American author

SUMMARY

▪ You are the person you are, largely as a result of your life experiences.

▪ Practise the 'eight steps to success' to remain empowered in any situation.

▪ Decide on a name that reflects the New You.

▪ Find the joy in your everyday life to achieve the balance between moving towards your long-term goals, yet also living in the moment.

Part 2

Developing the right skill set

This second part of the book is packed full of practical skills and ideas for routines and habits that can be incorporated into your daily life to support your new positive mindset. Together, the right mindset and skills will provide you with everything you need to create a better kind of life for yourself.

08

The art of communication – the power of meaning

Do you find yourself becoming frustrated that people just don't seem to listen to you? Are there times when it feels like you're speaking 'Double Dutch' simply because others do the complete opposite to the instructions you've given? Do you feel that nobody gives any weight to your point of view? Then it's likely that your communication skills could do with improving. Effective communication does not happen by accident: with the right skills you'll be understood no matter who you are talking to and what the circumstances are.

I was first given the opportunity to manage a team of people at the relatively young age of 24. At the time I worked in London in a high-pressured environment and I had no managerial experience or managerial training. I was asked to manage a team of six experienced people, who all also happened to be older than me and predominantly male – just a small challenge then! All I had to rely on was my passion and enthusiasm, but little did I appreciate how important the art of good communication would become.

I can remember distinctly one particular day, not long after I had started in the job, when during a team meeting I had communicated an objective to all of the six team members, discussed resources, time scales and everyone had left with a very clear understanding of what was expected and what they had to do ... or so I thought. Imagine then my frustration when three days later I was presented with six variations of the task I'd asked for.

EFFECTIVE COMMUNICATION DOES NOT HAPPEN BY ACCIDENT: WITH THE RIGHT SKILLS YOU'LL BE UNDERSTOOD.

I can remember thinking: 'Muppets, these people are just Muppets if they can't carry out a simple task. Clearly they just weren't listening!' Not a great leadership mindset from me, but in that moment I was simply so frustrated that everyone in the team had not understood the clear simple instructions I had given.

Then came a moment of clarity and I realised that the art of communication is not what you say or how well you say it, it's how people respond and the meaning *they* associate with what you've said. It wasn't that the team weren't listening it was simply that they'd interpreted my instructions differently and then acted accordingly – it was my failure to communicate effectively.

Have you ever fallen out with someone, perhaps one of the people closest to you, your partner, a close family member, a dear friend? Or have you ever had an altercation or felt frustrated at work that someone was not listening, maybe your boss, another team member or even a client? About 99 per cent of all of miscommunications arise because either others interpret what we say differently than the way we intended, or because we've attached a different meaning to what's being said to us and then we act accordingly.

Finding the meaning in communication

To become better at communication it's worth understanding more about how we communicate with others and how we interpret the meaning behind what's being said. And it's not just about the words.

A newborn child is not born with the language skills of a grown adult, yet it is still able to bond with and identify its own mother through a highly developed sense of hearing and sense of smell. Any mother of a newborn will testify that a very upset baby, crying for no obvious reason, will often calm down once they are placed back in their mother's arms and the mother begins to talk or sing softly to her child.

Although babies make lots of noise from the start, language skills are in fact one of the last skills they develop, usually at around 18 months onwards as more cognitive brain patterns develop. Language development continues well into childhood. Communication through language comes along long after babies have learnt to sit up, walk, point, eat, draw and a whole raft of other skills. Yet, as any parent or carer of a small child will know, very young children are able to communicate using a dialogue made up of different cues other than language.

Is it any surprise, therefore, if we misinterpret the messages being communicated to us when we only use language cues to 'listen' to others? To master the art of communication we need to become much more aware of all the other cues that make up the whole picture.

Many studies have concluded that communication can be broken down into three key areas:

1 What we say.

2 How we say it.

3 Our body language as we say it.

However, I believe there is a fourth key to communication that is vitally important, which is *your intention* as you communicate with others. Remember it's all about how others interpret the *meaning* behind what you say, not what you say. So let's take each of these elements individually.

Key area 1: What we say

The words we choose are more a reflection of ourselves than the person we're speaking to. What we say verbally is a direct reflection of our 'self-talk', our own Vicky Pollard voice, and we choose words that have the appropriate amount of emotional intensity attached to them – for us. However, the words that we use may mean nothing to the other person, so the first big clue in communicating more effectively with others is to listen very carefully to their choice of language, then use *key phrases* that are relevant to them.

Think how much more difficult it is to communicate with someone who does not share the same first language as yourself. Even though it's possible to translate their words in your head, often the meaning is lost in the translation. If you don't believe me, try telling your favourite joke in a foreign language and I bet you won't receive many laughs from your audience!

Even in your own language there are huge variations between countries, regions, dialect and colloquial phrases. In a business environment often a cultural language will emerge that to any new employee can seem daunting. I once worked for a global business that had its own phrase book!

I spent a fabulous period of my life in my mid-20s living and travelling in New Zealand. As the only 'Pommie' amongst my group of 'Kiwi' friends my accent and choice of language provided much amusement. It didn't seem to matter how many times I pointed out that I was in fact *English*, born in *England* and was speaking the *English* language, and perhaps it could be *their* choice of words that they should be giggling at. Nope, every time I use the word 'swimming costume' as opposed to 'togs', or 'flip flops' instead of 'jangles' that would be it, everyone falling around in fits of laughter. Also, coming from the wet and wonderfully temperate climate of England, it was the only time in my life I'd ever heard the phrase 'Quick, shut the patio door – we need to keep the heat *out!'*

However, the words we use are also a reflection of something known as our own *primary representational system,* which is scientific speak for what basically means the main way in which our brains store up and then *re-present* information. There are three ways people tend to use to store and talk about information – *visual, auditary* and *kinaesthetic,* sometimes referred to as the VAK system.

The VAK system
Visual

Visual thinkers make sense of their world visually, which means if you are talking to them, they may not be able to retain information if it is only communicated verbally, even if they appear to be listening very hard. After about 10 seconds their brain goes on mute and they can't retain the audio information. To compensate for this they will have a desire to write things down and they love pictures, colours, charts, graphs or any visual representations of the same information. In a business environment I can often spot the visual thinkers immediately as they are the team members who are constantly armed with 'pen and paper' – they never leave their desks without them!

YOU NEED TO TURN UP YOUR SENSORY ACUITY IN ORDER TO PICK UP ON ANY 'VISUAL' CUES.

It's easy to spot these people when you meet them if you have your 'Scooby ears' pricked up. You need to turn up your sensory acuity in order to pick up on any 'visual' cues.

As well as writing and drawing, as you talk to them visual thinkers talk very, very quickly, usually in an animated manner. They use their hands and lots of gestures when speaking. I'm a highly visual thinker and I can remember when I was a child my Granny making me sit on my hands to keep me quiet. I absolutely lost all ability to speak at that point as I find it so hard to talk if I'm not moving my hands. However, the easiest clue to decide if a person is visual is to listen to their choice of words, as their language will be peppered with visual references such as:

- 'I *see* what you mean.'
- 'That *looks* good to me.'
- 'Let me *show* you.'
- 'Do you get the *picture*?'

If you're communicating with someone who has a visual style, first think of the environment you're in, as they will become easily distracted by changes in their peripheral vision, yet often respond well to 'white noise' in the background and prefer that to complete silence. So, for example, if you have a primary style of visual you are much more likely to want the radio on in the background, regardless of whether you are at work or are pottering about your home.

Someone with this style would much prefer any communication

to be supported with visual references, so draw your explanation or use a picture. Finally, include visual language when you speak, since when you say, 'Let me show you', unconsciously a visual thinker's brain will be taking a big sigh of relief and thinking, 'Yes! no translation required'.

I can remember once taking a call from my good friend Colin who asked me a particular question, to which I remember I responded, 'OK let me show you', and Colin was tickled pink that I was going to *show* him the answer over the telephone. Likewise I know that if I'm taking a call, say whilst I'm driving, I either have to pull over to write notes or ask the caller to email me the key points of the conversation as I'm unable to retain the information more than a few seconds after the call has ended.

Audio

The next style in the VAK system is known as auditory. Unlike the visual thinkers, people who have an auditory primary representational system make sense of their world through sound, and again they exhibit some key characteristics.

A person with an auditory style has a much more paced rhythmical pattern to their flow of speech compared to people with a visual style. Audios *love* the sounds of words and will use an elaborate vocabulary to express themselves. One of the biggest clues to picking up on their style is to again listen to the language that the person uses. So whereas a visual person is likely to say, 'Let me *show* you', an audio person will instead say, 'Let me *tell* you'. Some more examples of audio-styled language include:

- *'Listen* to this.'
- 'I *hear* you.'
- *'Sounds* like a plan.'
- 'That *rings* a bell.'

This kind of person prefers just to be told the information.

Diagrams, pictures and charts overcomplicate the information as far as they are concerned. So a person with this style would prefer a verbal explanation – they do not feel the need to make notes or write things down. Unlike the visuals, background noise drives the audios crazy and in order to think clearly they prefer peace and quiet.

I remember explaining this to a group once, and at this point the general manager of a hotel threw his hands up in the air and exclaimed, 'That's why he's like that!' It turns out that the person in question was this hotel manager's head chef. Every morning they would have a logistics meeting to discuss the events of that day, stock levels and any other points of business. The general manager would turn up to the meeting with pen and paper, printouts of any relevant figures and lots of diagrams to work through. Whereas the head chef would simply turn up to the meeting, sit down and fold his arms. He never took any notes yet was able to answer every question accurately and could repeat back verbatim every detail of the meeting.

The general manager used to find this exasperating and thought the head chef was simply trying to prove a point. Clearly the general manager had a primary representational system of visual, whereas the head chef was auditory in style. Even if the chef had taken notes in the meeting, once he'd referred back to them later, they wouldn't have helped. His brain would be recalling the words and sounds of the meeting.

Kinaesthetic

The final style is known as kinaesthetic and although this style is not as common as the previous two styles the clues are distinct – and with your Scooby ears perked up, relatively easy to spot. Anyone with a kinaesthetic primary communication style is very internally referenced and in tune with how things feel physically. Their brains make sense of their world by using muscle memory and by moving their bodies.

Kinaesthetic cues are very distinctive; as although kinaesthetic minds may be working overtime because they are so internally referenced, often these people struggle to put into words what they are thinking. This means that, to the other styles, they sometimes appear to be distant or detached. They may even have very breathy speech, a verbal reflex such as a 'humm' or 'ermm', or even a slight stutter.

Compared to the other two styles, kinaesthetics have a very, *very*, slow pace of speech, which can often frustrate the other styles – particularly the visuals who babble away at an enormous rate of knots. Kinaesthetic language makes references to *connection*, be that an inner connection or a connection with the physical environment. For example:

- 'get a *hold* of'
- '*tap* into'
- 'I have a *sense for*'
- 'make *contact*'
- '*catch* on'.

If you find yourself communicating with a kinaesthetic person, it's important that they interact physically as much as possible, as that is how their brains store information, make sense of it and then recall from memory.

A few years ago I came across a team of IT programmers who were so frustrated with one of the individuals on the team, as although he would *say* 'Yes' whenever they asked him if he understood what was required, he would consistently make what they considered to be silly little mistakes, which in previous discussions they had already identified and eliminated prior to the execution. Once they appreciated he had a kinaesthetic style they were able to allow him to work through his execution, understanding and building up the *feel* of the programming as he went along.

Which style are you?

Now at this point it's likely that you've begun to identify which is the style you believe to be your primary representational system. If you're still wondering, ask yourself how you prefer to be given information. If your natural inclination is to write things down, to make lists and you are drawn to visual references, then it's likely you are more visual. Whereas if you are able to remember a long list of verbal instructions – can someone tell you a big list of items to collect at the supermarket, and you're able to hold that information in your head? – then you are more inclined to be auditory in style. If you notice that you have a very slow pace of speech and other annoyingly impatient people, i.e. the visuals, keep finishing your sentences for you, or that you only truly understand something after you've done it, then it's likely that your preferred style is kinaesthetic.

However, you may be thinking, 'Actually I feel an affinity to each style and relate to more than one type of characteristic'. In this case you have a big advantage, as one of the key skills in being able to communicate more effectively with others is to use *that person's* preferred style. In fact it's less important which style you are, it's more about being flexible in your communication to match the cues of the other person.

It's also possible to use different styles in different scenarios and with different people. For example, my natural style is

IT'S POSSIBLE TO USE DIFFERENT STYLES IN DIFFERENT SCENARIOS AND WITH DIFFERENT PEOPLE.

visual yet my husband's natural style is kinaesthetic so I often find myself becoming more kinaesthetic the moment I step across the threshold when I arrive home.

Learn to adapt your style to that of the other person and you will instantly become more easily understood, reducing the chance of any miscommunication.

Key area 2: How we say it

When you're listening to someone speak, what has a greater impact: the words they use, or the tone of voice in which they're speaking? Of course, it's the tone of their voice. You could be giving the nicest compliment to someone, but if you use a sarcastic tone of voice as you speak to them, they will interpret the meaning as exactly that – sarcastic. Long after the words have been forgotten, the hidden messages in the tone of voice will remain.

Malcolm Gladwell, in his book *Blink*, refers to a study carried out with medical professionals in the US, looking for any correlation between doctors who were sued more often than the national average and those doctors who had never been sued. After they had eliminated all the obvious correlations such as bad practice or missed diagnoses – as well as the less obvious such as age, gender, geography, place of study, none of which showed any correlation – they extended their research to include other factors. In a highly scientific study, they analysed 10-second slices of 'white noise' doctor/patient conversations where the detail of the words could not be heard, only the tone of the doctor's voice. Guess what? The biggest factor that would determine whether a doctor is likely to be sued in America is not the quality of the care they offer, it's the tone of voice they use when dealing with their patients! In fact the study actually showed that in some cases where doctors had indeed been negligent, if they had treated their patients with empathy, concern and interest, the patients would shift any blame on to someone else rather than blame that doctor.

Clearly the tone of your voice is going to have a huge impact on how others interpret the meaning in your message.

My mother runs a children's dancing school and I grew up teaching little ones to be beautiful butterflies or fairy princesses. When communicating with the smaller children I adopted a very animated, almost sugary tone of voice to engage their interest and make everything sound exciting. However, when I started in big business I wasn't aware that I was using the same tone of voice, which to a group of adults sounds completely patronizing. Fortunately, someone pointed this out to me and, after watching myself on video, I was absolutely horrified.

So, if you are frustrated that others do not appear to be listening to you or taking you seriously then I suggest you also become aware of the tone of your voice. There is, for example, a big difference between coming across as aggressive as opposed to assertive, or dictatorial as opposed to commanding respect. So if you feel that you are not getting the response you'd hoped for from the people you are communicating with, then either ask for some honest feedback from someone you trust or record yourself so that you can hear the tone of your own voice – you may be surprised, just as I was.

Key area 3: Our body language as we say it

The choice of words and the tone of voice we use are important in communication, but the next element has even *more* impact on the meaning when we communicate.

How hard can it be?

A couple of years ago a popular TV advert for *The Yellow Pages* phone directory featured an uncle who had been asked to take his niece to the hairdressers. Instead he attempted the hair cut himself, saying the immortal words, 'How hard can it be?' He soon found out how hard it could be, as he made a terrible mess of the poor girl's hair.

When the mother returned home to see the awful mess on the top of her daughter's head, she insisted they go straight back to the hairdressers (which in fact they had never visited in the first place). With the mother waiting in the car, and watching through the window, the uncle frogmarched his niece into the hairdressers, where the mother can see him tearing a strip off the receptionist, pointing at the girl's hair and clearly insisting that they remedy the terrible mess immediately. Mum looked satisfied. In fact, what we can hear but Mum can't is that the uncle was actually telling the receptionist that they are 'very, very nice people', and if they sorted out the mess he had created, he would pay them double!

What made the advert so funny and striking was the mismatch between the body language of the uncle, as seen by the mother, and his actual words. Small wonder the receptionist just stared at him open mouthed. The key point is: even though the mother couldn't hear a word of the conversation, just from watching the uncle's body language she was absolutely satisfied that he was doing exactly as she asked. That's the power of body language in communication.

The way we move as we speak has more impact on the interpretation than words and tonality combined! So even if you only make one small change in your behaviour and you become more aware of the subliminal messages you send out via your body, this alone will have a big impact on how others perceive what you say.

Think of someone you admire, or who has earned your respect, maybe someone you work with or a personal acquaintance. Why is it that you feel that way about that person? When they speak do people listen? Often it is the quiet leader whom people choose to listen to. Everyone can remember a teacher at school who could silence a rowdy class by simply entering the room and standing there. Similarly there was also the teacher who would shout and scream at their noisy pupils, who would continue to blatantly ignore the teacher and carry on causing a riot in the classroom. Why? Because that teacher did not project the necessary authority through their body language and no one took their words seriously.

Simply turning up the volume and shouting louder to control an out-of-control situation usually has the opposite effect – *you* end up out of control.

Even if you are not in front of the person you are talking to, they can still pick up on your body language. It is possible to 'hear' a smile down the phone, just as you can detect apathy, boredom and disinterest. So you may need to change your body language even when speaking over the phone. Stand up if you need to project more authority in your voice. Evoke the appropriate body language and you'll immediately strengthen the message in your communication.

Key area 4: Your intentions

Finally, the last piece of the jigsaw in communicating more effectively isn't even something you say or do, it's your intentions as you interact with others. Whether you are aware of it or not, what you are thinking will come across subliminally to the other person.

Recently I initiated a group exercise, the purpose of which was to 'read' the other person's communication cues. During the feedback session, one of the delegates commented that although their buddy *appeared* to be interested in what they were saying, they just knew it was an act. And all credit to the buddy who admitted that at the time they had been thinking, 'Oh help, he's boring'. You won't often get this kind of frank feedback, but whether you are aware of it or not, you will transmit your thoughts and emotions to others.

Typically women are better at picking up on this than men, which is why when a husband says to his wife, 'Yes darling, I am listening', when in fact he has one eye on the football scores appearing on the TV over his wife's shoulder – she knows he's not listening to her! Just as the customer who knows the salesperson is thinking more about their commission than the benefits to them the customer, or the boss who doesn't particularly like one team member. It's hard to think something while talking without other people picking up on it.

This brings us once again full circle to the importance of developing the right psychology first, before fine-tuning your communication skills. Think about what your outcome from the interaction is and use a power question to get you into the zone. For example, ask yourself 'What do I need to do or say now, to help this person understand?' or 'What information do I really need to understand from this customer, before I can persuade them to my point of view?'

WHETHER YOU ARE AWARE OF IT OR NOT, WHAT YOU ARE THINKING WILL COME ACROSS SUBLIMINALLY TO THE OTHER PERSON.

Whether it's at work or with family, a bit of effort to communicate better improves every area of your life and can produce very noticeable results.

SUMMARY

- The art of communication is more about the meaning that others associate with what you said than what you believe you've said.

- The meaning behind what we say is made up of:

  - the words we use

  - our tone of voice

  - how we move when we speak

  - our intentions when we communicate.

- Everyone uses a strategy of either visual, auditory or kinaesthetic (VAK) primary representational systems to store and then represent information.

- If we pick up on someone's cues then we can easily adapt our own behaviour to improve the effectiveness of our communication.

09

Positive relationships – the power of connection

I recently watched a film called *Into the Wild*, which recounts two years of the life of Christopher McCandless, a young man who following his graduation decides to adopt a new identity and a bohemian lifestyle, living on the road with no attachments to either people or anything materialistic. His only ambition is to venture into the wilds of Alaska, which he believes to be the ultimate freedom. He's successful in doing so, but having achieved his goal there is a poignant moment in the film when Christopher writes in his journal that 'life is for sharing'. At that moment he realizes how much he misses his fellow man.

The human experience is ultimately about connection with others. Learning how to develop strong, meaningful relationships is a great skill to have, yet one that is not often taught. In this chapter we're going to look at building strong, meaningful relationships in two areas: firstly, how to build the best personal relationship with your partner (and how to attract them in the first place if you aren't already in a relationship); and secondly how to build a great relationship with strangers. Let's start with the most important first.

Creating the perfect relationship with a partner

Creating a perfect relationship may not be high up on your agenda right now, especially if you are single (by your own choice or not), but ultimately finding a mate with whom together you build your perfect lives can only magnify your own personal success and emotional joy.

If you're reading this chapter and you are already in a relationship, then focus on how you could make that relationship even better. If you're single and would ideally prefer to be in a relationship, then use this chapter as preparation for creating your perfect relationship.

One of the biggest mistakes many people make before they even get involved with someone is that they don't first decide what it is they want, instead they fall for the person who happens to show up! Initially their rose-tinted glasses cloud their vision, making them believe that the other is the perfect partner. Then six months later, by which point they are much more emotionally and logistically invested in the relationship, the glasses slide off and they realize that the other person is not 'The One'.

Decide first, attract second

So step one in creating your perfect relationship is first to decide what it is you want from it – make a wish list just for this. You should be as specific as possible, noting everything that is important to you. What feelings would this relationship give you? Is age important to you? What about this person's life circumstances, immediate family, beliefs, career, financial circumstances, goals in life? If looks are important to you, then describe some of their key features.

You're not being shallow by making these choices, you are simply being clear. For example, I have a girl friend who is very tall, over 6 foot, and it was really important to her to find a partner who wasn't shorter than her. Another friend knew she didn't want to have children of her own, but would be happy to

STEP ONE IN CREATING YOUR PERFECT RELATIONSHIP IS FIRST TO DECIDE WHAT IT IS YOU WANT FROM IT.

become involved with someone who already had children, providing they don't live with him full time.

However, when you write your wish list pay the most attention to the qualities of your ideal person, the kind of person they are: circumstances can change in life but qualities may not. It helps if you are in a relationship with someone who shares similar beliefs to your own and who either has similar aspirations or a desire to support yours.

I did this exact same exercise after many unsuccessful years out in the dating wilderness. Less than three weeks later I met my perfect partner, who later became my husband. When I reflected back on the list I had written, he ticked all the boxes, yet the interesting thing is that previously I would have overlooked this opportunity, as he didn't come *packaged* in the same way that I'd previously looked for. Not that I didn't think he was attractive, but previously I'd always made a bee-line for the suited and booted types (you know the ones your mum always wanted you to end up with) and when I met Kevin he did a manual job without much in the way of prospects – and definitely no suit! However, when I looked back, that wasn't on my list – so clearly it hadn't been *that* important to me. The interesting thing is that five years later he has a completely different career, yet the qualities for which I love him are still the same.

What kind of person do you need to be?

The second part of perfecting the most awesome relationship is to then consider what type of person *you* need to be in order to either attract or draw out of someone the qualities you desire most.

Your intimate relationship should be the most important relationship you have in your life, yet it's usually the one we pay the least attention to. We lash out at the person who really deep down we want to support and then become defensive if they lash back, or feel disappointed if they become withdrawn.

So instead decide how you can be the perfect partner for them. What do they need? When you give selflessly to your partner you will draw out the same qualities within them. So if there are times when you feel you're not getting what *you'd hoped* for, instead of focusing on what you're not getting,  switch your focus to what *they need*. Remember the lightbulb analogy: you want this person in your life shining so brightly, everyone notices, especially when they do the same for you too. You both fill each other up.

Uncover their emotional needs

If your goal is to make your partner happy, then you need to work out how you can do that. It's likely that you will work out some of your partner's emotional needs by simply observing their behaviour (remember when someone is under pressure, they increase the intensity of their behaviour, which gives you more clues). It's important to know how through your own behaviour you can fulfil those needs – obviously in a positive, empowering way that makes both you and them feel good.

One of the prerequisite emotions that everyone wants to feel in a relationship is the feeling of being *loved*. Now, you could continue your lives together, best-guessing and observing how they respond to your behaviour – or you could simply ask them.

It helps if you create the mood for this type of conversation as it's not one to have when the kids are running riot or you're both exhausted from a long day at work. Instead, arrange to go out for dinner – with the purpose of talking about how you can make your relationship even better. Then ask your partner, 'What would you like to feel more of, and what do I do or can I do more of that makes you feel like that?'

I remember having this conversation with my husband whilst on holiday, in a beautiful restaurant overlooking the sea, and I had just reeled off a big list of things like, 'I love it when you surprise me with small notes or unexpected gifts, it makes me feel appreciated. I love it when you take our son out for an hour or two leaving me to have a quiet soak in the bath ...' and so on. You can see how the conversation was going.

However, when it was my turn to ask him I was completely gob-smacked at his response. He simply requested, 'Answer the phone'. My response was, 'And what else?' to which he said, 'That's it honestly. Just answering the phone when it rings would make me feel so loved and appreciated.'

At the time Kevin dealt with telephone calls from the public all day long. It so happened that his favourite seat at home was next to the home phone. So previously whenever it rang, I would dig him in the ribs and say 'Well, answer it then!'. No matter how well I thought I knew him, there was no way I would have worked that one out without some help.

So now every time the phone rings in our house, I leap up, run across the room and shout, 'I'll get it', and it's great to see the smile spread across his face.

Agree the boundaries

The final element in attracting and creating your perfect relationship is to agree early on the boundaries that are important to you both, as this builds trust and mutual respect.

So, for example, is it OK to be late home, providing that you check in and let the other person know? I can remember times spent socializing with friends when some people would switch their mobile phones off so that they didn't see the messages piling up from their partners asking where they were when they were late. That never made sense to me. It's OK by me if plans change, providing that you are considerate to your partner and let them know.

What's allowed when you communicate, particularly when you have a disagreement? Is it acceptable to you both to scream and shout inappropriately, then make up passionately, or do you agree that you will never raise your voices?

Finally, it's important to check in regularly. It does not take long at all for a relationship to start to turn sour, and most people bury their heads in the sand and hope things will get better on their own, when in fact if you do not stay tuned in, there is only one way the relationship can go – and that's down.

YOU MAY BE IN DANGER OF REPEATING THE SAME RELATIONSHIP AGAIN AND AGAIN ONLY WITH A DIFFERENT PERSON.

Your intimate relationship is probably the best opportunity to learn about yourself. If a relationship doesn't work out for some reason, before you embark on the next one, take some time to reflect and decide what your responsibilities to the overall outcome were, and what you can and *will do* differently next time. Otherwise you may be in danger of repeating the same relationship again and again only with a different person each time.

Creating great relationships with absolutely anybody

The ability to meet somebody for the first time and quickly build up a strong connection is one of those things that we believe we are simply born with (or not), and which comes naturally to some and not others. Well, the good news is that, no matter how easy or difficult you find it to connect with people, there are some very simple techniques you can use to create a connection with anyone.

Wouldn't it be great if you only ever had to deal with people who you naturally liked? No more challenging family relationships, no more demanding customers to deal with and no more tense situations with colleagues, with whom you don't see eye to eye.

Clearly that's not going to happen, so instead we have to learn how to connect with people no matter who they are, what they do or where they come from. So how do you do it? The good news is that like most 'life skills' this is something you do already with the people you naturally like, so you simply need to relearn these techniques and apply them to those relationships that are more challenging.

There are four things to bear in mind as you aim to build a connection with someone.

1 Your desired outcome

What do you want to achieve in building this relationship? So, for example, if you work in sales and want to build a connection with a customer, you might be thinking, 'How can I cream as much as possible out of this sale so that I can achieve a bonus?' or instead, 'I wonder how I can achieve the best possible outcome for myself and my customer?' Just as in the last chapter, whatever your intentations are, I guarantee the customer will detect it. They will be able to pick up on your desired outcomes by using their own Scooby ears and they are less likely to be open to you if they know your intentions are purely selfish.

2 Perk up those Scooby ears

This is definitely the time to make sure your Scooby ears are well and truly perked up. It's really important when you're aiming to build a better connection with someone that you are using all of your sensory acuity to *read* the other person and how they are reacting to you. If you want to know what meaning they are associating with your behaviour, your Scooby ears will tell you.

3 Be flexible

If the other person is not responding to you in the way that you'd hoped, then it's up to *you* to modify your behaviour. Remember, it's the person with the most behavioural flexibility that achieves their preferred outcome, particularly if your intentions are pure and positively focused.

4 Develop a healthy curiosity

Develop a healthy curiosity about the other person, their thinking and behaviour, rather than being judgemental. When something doesn't add up or make sense to you, that doesn't mean it's wrong – it's just different. If you agree that we are largely a product of our environment then it makes sense that people from diverse backgrounds, cultures, education and religions will have different views and opinions. If your intention is to make a connection with that person, the minute you form a judgement of them you are only comparing them and their behaviour with your perception of what is right and wrong (i.e. your filters come into play).

Instead, develop a healthy curiosity about that person and their opinions; this means you remain open to their point of view. This doesn't mean you have to agree with them or change your own opinions, only that you respect that they may have a different point of view. The minute you form your judgement of someone is the minute you lose the ability to connect with them.

However, as is often the case, this is so much easier said than done.

Being judgemental – a test from the universe

I can remember a time when I was in America and two of my friends made a commitment that they would not form a judgement of anyone ever again. I love the way that the universe comes along with a big whack! to test you, usually just after you've made a pretty big commitment like that, as if to say, 'Come on, are you serious? Well here's a test just to make sure.'

The very next day they spotted an oriental-looking man driving on the wrong side of the road causing traffic chaos, clearly endangering himself and everyone else in the vicinity. On observing this man's behaviour, my friends would usually have made some derogatory comment about his driving, perhaps even linking it to his ethnicity. However, with their new-found commitment to remain curious rather than forming judgements, instead they flagged him down, and discovered he wasn't from the US, but a businessman visiting from Japan where they drive on the opposite side of the road. The different road layouts, traffic signals and road signs in a different language had simply overwhelmed the gentleman and they discovered that he was in quite a distressed state.

If my two friends had been judgemental about the Japanese man, they would have been unlikely to connect with him. Instead their curiosity meant they were able to identify he was in trouble, were able to stop him being a danger to himself and others, and they were able to guide him to safety.

There is no such thing as a *bad* person, only ever *bad* behaviour. Remain curious about a person's behaviour rather than negatively label them based on their behaviour.

Building rapport

What is *rapport?* Some people would describe it as the feeling you have when you just seem to 'click' with someone. With some people (usually those we like) we seem to have natural rapport, yet with others the relationship can feel unnatural and uncomfortable. So why is it rapport seems to be easier with the people you like? Because we like people who are like us.

Watch couples flirting with each other in a bar or club. As they build rapport you will notice the subtle changes that occur between them. They'll be standing in mirrored body shapes; they each take a drink from their glass at the same time. Unconsciously they are sending each other subtle signals that will make the other person more comfortable, and create a bond. This works because we feel an affinity with people who we believe are like us, so by unconsciously standing the same way as they do, or mirroring their behaviour, we're sending a message that says, 'Hey look, I'm just like you'. At the other end of the spectrum,

THERE IS NO SUCH THING AS A *BAD* PERSON, ONLY EVER *BAD* BEHAVIOUR.

you might have witnessed that moment when someone tries to build rapport with a person, perhaps again in a social situation, and the other person gives them the 'cold' shoulder, clearly not wanting to build rapport or indeed a connection.

Building rapport is something you already unconsciously know how to do – it's just a question of becoming aware of how you do it, so that you can replicate the techniques when you actively *need* to build rapport, perhaps in a business situation, or in a social setting where you don't know anyone.

The simplest rapport-building technique is known as *matching and mirroring* and quite simply involves copying or reflecting the other person's subtle signals. Remember, this is something that you do already when you naturally feel comfortable with someone, so all you are doing here is understanding what you do and applying it to someone you want to build a connection with.

Let's look at some of these signals in more detail.

The VAK system

In the last chapter we talked about visual, audio and kinaesthetic people and each of their key characteristics. When building rapport with someone, you can simply mirror the characteristics of their particular VAK system. It'll make them feel more comfortable and help you connect.

Voice qualities

This is one you probably won't need to try too hard to master as it's normal to match and mirror someone's voice, without any conscious effort. If you meet someone who talks very quietly and you are a naturally loud person, it's likely you would adjust your volume to match that of the person you are talking to. The same philosophy applies to pace, pitch and tone.

I'm a Geordie lass from the north-east of England and we Geordies have a very distinctive accent, as well as a naturally fast-paced speech. I remember when I first moved to London I spoke so quickly nobody could understand a word I was saying, so in order to be understood I naturally started to match the pace and rhythm of other people's speech and I s-l-o-w-e-d down.

Language

Remember in the last chapter we highlighted the importance of the words we choose in great communication? And that what we say is a direct reflection of what we think? Therefore, if you want to build a connection with someone, it's crucial to use *their* language. That means you need to listen to what they say and the words they use, then slot them back into your speech.

When I'm working with a client and ask a question, then record their answers, I'm very observant and ensure I only use their language and not my interpretations of their language. So, for example, if someone says 'I struggle making sales calls', I record exactly what they've said, even if in my head I could interpret the same phrase as 'I find sales calls difficult'. Do these two phrases mean the same thing? The answer is, no, not to the person who said, 'I struggle making sales calls', as those particular words have a particular emotional meaning to that person. So, the next time you have a conversation with someone, really listen to the phrases they use, not your interpretations or the words that you would use.

Body shape

Whether you're sitting or standing together, pay attention to the other person's stance and then mirror them. Are their hands in or out of their pockets? Do they stand on one leg or centred? What is the angle of their shoulders and head?

If you are sitting down, do. they have their legs crossed or uncrossed? How do they have their hands placed? Are they leaning forward or relaxed back in their chair? Mirror their body shape exactly and you will build rapport quickly and easily.

Gestures

Very often people have gestures they develop that are particular to them. When they speak, how do they emphasise a point? Do they clasp their hands together, or place one hand out in front? Pay attention to any specific gestures, then use them in your conversation. I remember once working with someone who used his right index finger to simultaneously tap the end of the fingers on his left hand as he was speaking. I mirrored this and I swear I thought his eyes were going to pop out of his head, as unconsciously he seemed to be thinking, 'Wow, she's a finger tapper just like me'.

Breathing

This is probably one of the most subtle cues you can use to build rapport but possibly one of the most powerful. When we breathe at a certain rhythm and pace, our energy vibrates at the same rhythm and pace as the other person's, and when you can connect with someone at an energy level you can build a powerful connection very quickly.

If you've ever felt someone's presence as they've entered a room, particularly before you've seen them, then you've felt their energy or their 'aura'.

Now this is not an excuse to stare inappropriately at someone's chest! But if you can tune into the pace and rhythm of that person's breathing then your energy will become in sync and the other person will instantly feel much more comfortable with

PAY ATTENTION TO ANY SPECIFIC GESTURES, THEN USE THEM IN YOUR CONVERSATION.

you. Remember we like people who are like us, so the more that we become like the other person, the more rapport they will feel with us.

If this is completely new to you, then you might be feeling a bit concerned, even worried that you'll end up looking silly in your attempts to mirror the other person, or that there's something a bit false about copying people's body language. Firstly, remember this is something that you unconsciously do anyway when you yourself feel comfortable with someone; it's a perfectly natural thing to do. Secondly, being relaxed is the key. Make small adjustments and naturally mirror as you talk to the other person – that way it won't feel like you are copying them.

Trust me, try it out and you will see how easy it is to create strong rapport: it only takes around 10 seconds to build rapport.

Pace and lead

You know you have achieved strong rapport when the other person starts to copy you! This is what is known as *pace and lead* and is a natural process when someone feels an affinity with you. They do say imitation is the highest form of flattery.

Watch out for pace and lead as a signal for how much rapport you've created. Try purposely changing your body language and see if the other person copies you. If so, you can feel confident that they feel an empathy with you.

It's also the way to work out who is the rapport leader in a group scenario. Watch the body language of the other people and see whose body language they're copying. One of my clients is a Japanese manufacturing firm and there is one Japanese manager who has quite a distinctive gesture of twiddling his pen. In team meetings, if someone else wants to get the attention of the group just before making a point, they will start to twiddle their pen in exactly the same way. Before you know it all 12 team members are simultaneously twiddling pens, wanting to gain control of the group's rapport.

If you find yourself in this type of situation, mirror the rapport leader first, and you will then automatically be able to lead the other members of the group.

Be interested, rather than interesting

I have yet to meet anyone who does not like talking about themselves! In most conversations we're more interested in talking about ourselves than really paying attention to the other person. At best, we seek to find some common topic which we have some affinity with, so that we can respond by talking about our experience, opinion or story.

The next time you meet someone, aim to spend 80 per cent of the conversation focused on them. Ask them questions, probe them for their opinions and every time they ask you a question, turn it round again, inviting them to share even more information about themselves.

"You can make more friends in two months by becoming interested in other people than you can in two years trying to get other people interested in you."

Dale Carnegie, American author

While writing this book, one day Saturday afternoon I was standing in my local bookshop idly looking at various titles in the same genre, when a man noticed that I had pulled out quite a number of books and asked, 'Do you read a lot of these types of books?' What a corker of an opening line for someone like me! I so easily could have ranted on about my passion for the subject, or the fact that I was indeed writing my own book, or about my business services – so much to talk about! Instead I mirrored him back and asked, 'I've read some. Do you read a lot of these types of books?'

In the conversation that ensued over the next 20 minutes, I continued to use the same technique to uncover a lot more about this man, asking where he was in his life. I made some recommendations that would fulfil his current needs and, best of all, we swapped business cards. Two weeks later he called me to ask if we could meet up and if he could join our coaching programme. Obviously, I was delighted at gaining the business but I was much more delighted that I had been able to make such a profound connection with a complete stranger in a bookshop. I'm not sure we would have achieved the same outcome if I'd answered his first question directly and made it 'all about me'.

The more you show interest in someone else, the more they will see you as an interesting person – someone who's easy to talk to and a nice person to have around.

SUMMARY

- Create your perfect relationship by:
  - deciding what you want out of your relationship
  - working out what kind of person you need to be, to either draw out those qualities in your partner or to attract your ideal partner
  - uncovering your partner's driving emotional needs and then discussing how each of you can fulfil them for the other

- agreeing the boundaries of your relationship, so that you are both clear of the expectations of the other person.

With new acquaintances, we connect most easily with people who are like ourselves.

Mirror all the small details of someone's behaviour to build rapport naturally with anyone.

When they copy you, it's a sign that you've achieved pace and lead, and they feel in rapport with you.

In conversation, be interested in order to be interesting, by placing the focus of your attention on the other person.

10

Become a master of influence – the power of persuasion

Why include a chapter on influencing skills in a book designed to help you lead a better life? Simply because it's unlikely that you will be able to achieve all of your wish list without enlisting the help of others, which is why knowing how to persuade and influence others is also a very powerful and necessary skill.

I guarantee somewhere in your life you need to be able to persuade others. Maybe your work involves some form of selling (in which case it's obvious) or perhaps you just need to get your children to tidy their bedrooms. Whether you're fundraising for your favourite charity, or getting your partner to agree to your redecoration plans, whether you need to persuade somebody to give you a new job, or are trying to set up your own business, every single one of us needs to influence and persuade others at some point, and the better we are at it, the more successful we'll be in life.

To be clear, we aren't talking about brainwashing or the hard sell or pressurising people against their will. Modern influencing is an art form – one that should be executed with grace and elegance, one that allows fruitful relationships to form and one that generates a win/win outcome for everyone.

Knowing how to become a master of influence will not only allow you to enrich your own life, but also give you the ability to help and benefit other people who are important to you. It will help you grow business, negotiate a harmonious family life,

MODERN INFLUENCING IS AN ART FORM – ONE THAT SHOULD BE EXECUTED WITH GRACE AND ELEGANCE.

raise well-balanced children and enlist others to help you achieve your goals even faster.

The power of persuasion – a new definition

It's not only salespeople (who use persuasion skills as part of their job) who are really good at influencing others. When you influence someone, what you actually do is get them to see things from your point of view, and when someone agrees with you, they are much more likely to follow your request or instructions – which is ultimately why being able to influence others is important. When you can combine your time and energy together with someone else's time and energy, your combined efforts create more momentum, which allows everyone to achieve their goals much more quickly.

Think about how all kinds of people are involved in influencing others in some form or another:

- a teacher who needs the attention of their pupils and to share their knowledge with the class
- a religious leader who shares their principles and beliefs with their congregation
- a parent who needs their child to adhere to the family and household standards and routines
- a business leader who needs everyone to buy into the company vision and strategy
- a man who's proposing to his girlfriend – he may be using a diamond ring as a *big* incentive but she has to believe that he will offer her unending wedded bliss!

All these are examples of influencing taking place in everyday situations and they all involve someone (or a group of people) coming round to another person's way of thinking. However, there is a fine line between becoming a master of influence and what I would call a 'conman', and that line is defined by your personal integrity. If your purpose in influencing someone is purely for your own means, the other person will know and they are less likely to agree with you.

Everyone at some time has experienced the uncomfortable pressure a salesperson (or indeed a member of your family) has put you under when they want to get their own way. It doesn't feel very nice. When you influence someone it should feel like a natural, enjoyable process for them; rather than feel pressure they should feel as if you have helped them out and you've had their best interests at heart.

What's in it for them?

The first element you need to think about if you want to persuade someone to your point of view is to think of it in terms of what they will gain: what's the benefit to them? This is a critical part of becoming a master influencer. Yet, in my experience, the one key that even the most experienced salespeople forget is the difference between *features* and *benefits*.

I have a little saying: *features tell – benefit sell.* Corny I know, but so true! A feature is what something does; the benefit is the difference it makes to the other person. The way I was originally taught the difference is to think of a briefcase and all the features that the briefcase may have, and then add 'which means' to convert those features into benefits. So for example:

- It has a handle *which means* it's easier to carry.
- There is a secure lock *which means* all your contents will be secure.
- It is made of quality leather *which means* it will enhance your image.

The same principle applies to anything you are hoping to persuade others to agree to; you must think about the benefit in terms of the other person.

- You want someone to support you on a project – why, what will it mean to them, what will they get out of it?

- You want your kids to tidy their bedrooms – how can you make them see that by doing so it really is a positive benefit to them? (Perhaps because you won't ground them if they do!)

- You're hoping to raise some finance for a new business idea – why should someone give you the money, how will they benefit?

- You want to organize a social night out and you want people to come along – why should they?

You would be amazed how many people I come across in the corporate world who understand this principle yet fail to actually do it. If you have a job or you run a business, take a look at your company's website or brochure and see how many benefits you can spot in the first few pages. Usually it's jam-packed with features, all about how great we are, this is what we do and what other people say about what we do; yet it has very little content about what all of that actually means for a potential customer. Unless you state your proposition in terms of both features and benefits you are effectively saying to any potential clients, 'I am a catalogue, have a flick through and pick your own benefits!'

Of course all this becomes much easier the more you understand about the other person – what makes them tick and why they would be interested in what you have to say or offer.

Find the hot button

The *hot button* is the key to influencing anybody with anything. If you can uncover the other person's motivation (and real reasons behind their motivation), you've found their hot button and got to the heart of why they would even consider coming round to your way of thinking. Armed with this insight, you are in a much more influential position to present your ideas or proposition in a way that is designed to fulfil the person's driving emotions and ultimately help them achieve their goals as well as yours.

There are three things to bear in mind as you dig to uncover someone's hot button. Uncover all three and you will have all the information you need. Don't panic, however, if for some reason that's not possible – perhaps because you don't know the person very well and they don't yet have full rapport with you. The more information you can gather, the more clues you have.

1 Their wants

Think about what drives the person. What are their goals, what do they *want* to achieve? What experiences in their life have shaped them into the person that they are today? All these factors will affect what it is they *think* they want. However, very often, as we will discover next, their wants are vastly different from what they actually *need*. So it's important to use your Scooby ears to work out what makes this person tick, but then also to find out what they really need.

2 Their needs

A person's *needs* are their emotional reasons why they want something. If they were to accept your proposition, what would they want to feel? Remember in Chapter 2 when you uncovered your own driving emotions which drive your behaviour – what does this other person really *need* and how can you help them achieve those feelings? Uncovering the driving emotions as to why someone would benefit from your proposal is crucial if you are to become a master influencer.

Think about a time when you agreed to something: whether that was something tangible you bought or something you agreed to, I guarantee the moment you made the decision to make the commitment was the moment you associated a feeling of ownership with that product, service or whatever that person made you feel.

If you own your own home, which in most people's lives is the biggest financial commitment they make, you can appreciate the importance of how things feel. When you go to see the estate agent, you usually have a checklist of requirements in your head and a budget in mind. Yet you won't buy a home unless it *feels* right, no matter how many boxes it ticks.

3 Their pain

Just as it's important to understand the emotional pleasure the other person will potentially gain from your proposition, it's equally important to understand what their potential *pain* would

IF YOU CAN UNCOVER THE OTHER PERSON'S MOTIVATION YOU'VE FOUND THEIR HOT BUTTON.

be. This means understanding what would be the consequence to the other person if they didn't take up your offer. As we discussed previously, in terms of your own personal drivers the strongest motivator is always to avoid pain, and the same is also true when we are aiming to influence someone else. When they associate more pain with *not* doing whatever you're suggesting, that's the moment they will make a commitment. So if they feel that they may lose out, and they feel a sense of loss, that's when they'll be really motivated to agree almost anything with you!

I once encountered a woman with a 'shoe problem'. She admitted to hiding six new pairs in her car, all purchased in the past 48 hours! She daren't take them into her house as she would then have to explain to her boyfriend where they'd come from!

I then proceeded to go on a fishing trip and ask her a series of questions to uncover her real reasons for buying the latest pair of shoes. The conversation went something like this. See if you can spot her hot button that kept making her buy shoes.

Nicola: So why did you buy that particular pair of shoes?

Woman: Because they looked nice.

Nicola: OK, but why that particular pair?

Woman: Because they were a good price.

Nicola: How much were they?

Woman: Only £45.00. [Expressed with huge emphasis on *only*.]

Nicola: Was that a good price?

Woman: Oh yeah, they should have been £79.99 but were reduced in the sale.

Nicola: Were you looking for a particular pair of shoes that day?

Woman:	No, not really, I was just filling time on my lunch hour.
Nicola:	So what made you decide you had to have that particular pair of shoes in your lunch hour?
Woman:	Because they were *so* pretty.
Nicola:	Why was that important?
Woman:	[Long pause.] Because I liked them.
Nicola:	What specifically about that particular pretty pair of shoes made you choose to part with £45 and buy them there and then?
Woman:	[Long, long pause.]
Nicola:	Let me ask a different question. What if you'd decided to leave it, think before making the purchase and instead go back the next day?
Woman:	[Look of utter shock and sharp intake of breath.] There is no way I could have done that.
Nicola:	Why not?
Woman:	Because what if they were gone?
Nicola:	What then, what if they were gone?
Woman:	I would have to kill someone! [I'm sure she wouldn't have killed someone but at this point in the conversation, clearly she is revealing her emotional attachment to the outcome. All her previous answers were logical responses. The next question I asked revealed a really interesting insight towards uncovering her hot button.]
Nicola:	OK, so what if I had gone shopping with you in your lunch hour and had taken your money off you so you couldn't buy *anything* and strapped your arms to your body so you couldn't steal anything either. Yet we spent an hour looking

round the shops and then left without buying anything, how would that have felt? [At this point she looked at me as if I was an alien who had just landed from outer space!]

Woman: Are you mad? I couldn't possibly do that?

Nicola: How mad am I? Why couldn't you possibly do that?

Woman: Because that would be a complete *waste of my time*.

Ah ha! So the real reason she buys so many pairs of shoes has absolutely nothing to do with the shoes themselves, but the *pain* of not filling her time. In her mind, £45 for a pair of pretty shoes that were on sale was a small price to pay to avoid the consequences of not doing something with her precious lunch hour. She values her time more than spending money.

This woman's buying experience highlights the real motivators behind someone's buying decision. Most people only ever aim to make their influencing argument based on the superficial reasons someone may give – are you looking for value for money, were you looking for a particular pair of shoes? Some people don't even go that far! But this example shows once again that our decision making runs much deeper – to our emotions and our perceptions of what will help us move closer to pleasure and further away from pain.

Now if my objective in uncovering this woman's hot button had been to influence her, I now know that the underlying driver in her behaviour is the desire to avoid wasting time, and I would be able to present any proposition in a way that presses this particular button.

As it turned out I was simply able to help her identify why she felt so compelled to make so many purchases of products she logically knew she didn't need – and so then allow her to make a positive shift in her behaviour.

So no matter what the scenario – be it personal or professional – take some time to uncover that person's real drivers, their hot button. All it takes is the use of open questions, a lot of patience and an intention to want to help. Remember – when you've asked a question, let the other person respond. Very often we become uncomfortable with any pauses and instead jump in and want to help them by guessing what they will say. Don't do it, it's a bad habit. Let them finish what they were going to say. It's the only way you can be sure of what they are thinking.

"You can have everything in life you want, if you will just help other people get what they want."

Zig Ziglar, American motivational writer

Master your belief

If influencing is about getting someone to come round to your point of view, then you need to be crystal clear yourself about your own thinking, which is why it's important to be sure of your belief in three key areas.

1 Belief in yourself

It's virtually impossible to persuade others to your point of view if you do not have belief in yourself or faith in your own opinions.

Remember that what you feel drives your behaviour, which means that if you feel you lack confidence then others will be able to see that in your demeanour – and that will not instil any confidence in you or your message.

2 Belief in your message

Whether you're selling a product or service, an idea or suggestion, you absolutely must believe in what you sell. You are asking someone to place their faith and commitment in your proposition so that it has to have some benefit to the other person – otherwise you fall into the category of conman. You may win over the other person today, but it's unlikely they would ever come back to you, want you as their friend or refer any business to you.

The same is true of any kind of influencing. You must believe in the message you convey – if you don't, others will instantly know that you are a phoney.

3 Belief in the purpose of your message

If you're in business or you work for someone you must believe in the vision and purpose of the company – if you don't, you need to do some serious thinking about your future with the company. If you are a family, you must believe that it's possible to all work together and have a happy and harmonious family life.

When Martin Luther King Jr. delivered his famous 'I have a dream' speech from the steps of the Lincoln Memorial on 28 August 1963, he stated: 'I have a dream that my four little children will one day live in a nation where they will not be judged by the colour of their skin, but by the content of their character.' I'm sure his words would not have been so powerfully felt if he himself had not believed in his vision or at the very least believed in the *possibility* of his dream coming true.

So what's the bigger picture for you? How can enlisting the support of others in achieving your goals also enable them to achieve theirs?

HOW CAN ENLISTING THE SUPPORT OF OTHERS IN ACHIEVING YOUR GOALS ALSO ENABLE THEM TO ACHIEVE THEIRS?

Master your emotions

In the first part of this book we looked at achieving success by mastering your emotions through developing the right psychology. As we are all ultimately emotional beings, ensuring you are a master of your own emotions is not only important for you personally but also because people are able to pick up on your feelings when you are aiming to persuade them to your point of view.

Have you ever received a telesales call late at night to your home from one of the many call centres around the world? Usually these types of sales calls are from poorly trained, inexperienced staff who have little passion or desire for the product. Think about the emotions, even down a telephone line, that you pick up about the person phoning you. What are they feeling and do they care about you?

Usually you pick up that they really don't care about you or the product they are attempting to sell, and if you don't buy it, they'll simply move on to the next poor sucker on their list!

Similarly, if you're organizing a social event but you're not that enthusiastic about it, when you're inviting someone to come along, your influence will be diminished as your feelings will come across in your tone of voice and your body language –

they'll pick up on your emotions. They'll be thinking, 'Why should I bother – they obviously don't think it's going to be a very good night'. Whereas when you ooze excitement, they'll be much more attracted to your invitation.

But I'm not a natural

'I wasn't born with the gift of the gab' or 'I'm not a natural' are common excuses for many people when it comes to persuasion skills, but I know that everyone has the capability within themselves to become a great influencer. How do I know? Every adult was previously a small child, and toddlers are the best influencers on the planet! They have no concept of rejection so come armed with bags of natural confidence and will do anything to achieve their goals. They don't often have the same resources available to them as adults, but that does not deter them – they simply up the stakes, usually in their behaviour, until you give in!

My young son has just turned 2 and his latest thing is the sunroof in our car. He has worked out that there is a 'magic' button which when pressed miraculously reveals the sky. So every time we're in the car all he does is shout, scream and wail for the 'sky-open'. No matter how much I logically explain to him that it's too cold to have the sunroof open, or that it's raining and we'll all get wet, he keeps at it until my nerves give in and we press the *magic* button. He's using his powers of influence over me, to get me to agree to his way of thinking – that opening the sunroof, come rain or shine, is great fun! Oh to be 2 years old again – such simple pleasures!

Now I'm not suggesting at all that you revert back to toddler-like behaviour in order to influence others, but you were once a child and it was so simple in your world back then. If you wanted something, you didn't comprehend any reasons why you couldn't have it, so you just simply asked – with the expectation that it would be given.

In our grown-up world we must try and rediscover these levels of confidence when it comes to influencing others – but this time, as we've discussed in this chapter, in much more appropriate ways.

SUMMARY

- Becoming a master of influence is an important skill in creating a successful life.

- Modern influencing is a graceful art form, one that allows win/win relationships to form.

- Uncover the other person's hot button to find their true motivators, then offer your solutions in terms of fulfilling *their* emotional needs.

- Master your self-belief, belief in your message and belief in the purpose of your message.

- Everyone already has within them the confidence to become a master of influence.

11

Inspire and lead –
the power of commanding respect

In order to create your success, why is it also important to develop your leadership capabilities? Simply because success and leadership go hand in hand. Whether you need to gain the respect of your children, your partner, your peers or you have a business to run, being someone who others respect and follow is a prerequisite to you achieving your goals. So what is it that makes a great leader?

Leadership has nothing to do with a job title or the amount of responsibility that others may have placed upon you. I've met many people who have had a great deal of responsibility placed upon them, yet who failed to inspire or lead anyone. The only way they could make others follow them was by shouting and screaming or worse still by using force. In contrast, I've met other people who had virtually no formal responsibility, yet a huge amount of influence over their peers. They are the ones to whom others look to for hope or a solution when a crisis comes along.

Leadership has nothing to do with a job title and everything to do with the amount of influence you naturally have over others. Leadership can work on many levels, from the ability to lead large groups of people to leading another person in a one-to-one relationship. However, before you are able to influence others the first basic level of leadership is the ability to *lead yourself*. In order to uncover some of your natural leadership character-istics, it's helpful to think about leaders you admire.

LEADERSHIP HAS NOTHING TO DO WITH A JOB TITLE AND EVERYTHING TO DO WITH THE AMOUNT OF INFLUENCE YOU NATURALLY HAVE OVER OTHERS.

Which leaders do you admire?

Who do you admire? It's good question isn't it? It's the first question I ask anybody looking to improve their leadership skills and the answers are always enlightening.

Some people choose family members, some a teacher from school, some a boss they once had, while others choose people from history or popular culture. So ask yourself the same question and write down the five leaders who've most inspired you throughout your life. Just as in the examples below these could be people personal to you, or well-known people, or indeed a mixture of both.

Once you've picked your top five, then question *why* you've picked them. Why do they deserve to be on your list? Make a note and write down a short phrase to record your answers. Take a moment now before reading any further to record your answers next to the names you've picked.

Here are some other people's choices:

Person	Why I've picked them
A particular captain in the army	Because they believed in me before I believed in myself.
My Mum	Because she found herself in very difficult circumstances raising a family on her own, yet we were never aware of this when we were growing up.
Richard Branson	Because he never allowed his dyslexia to hold him back.
Winston Churchill	Because he united a nation in the face of adversity.
A teacher at school	Because I was a bit of a bad lad but she never gave up on me.

Interesting … No one has ever made it on to the list based on the success they personally achieved, it's always about the *type* of person they were, how they achieved their success, how they used a particular talent or skill, or perhaps how they dealt with a particular situation. Sometimes people pick the same person, but for entirely different reasons. Richard Branson, for example, is a regular choice, but usually for very different reasons.

So what about your list? Have a look at your notes and the reasons why the individuals are on your list. Usually what you've identified in that person is a particular *quality* they possess and that is what you've picked up on.

Here are examples of some of the qualities great leaders possess:

- vision
- focus
- optimism
- trust
- integrity
- taking ownership
- courage
- accountability

- fearlessness
- determination
- passion
- creativity
- humility
- empathy
- loyalty
- resourcefulness.

In Chapter 2 we discovered that what we see in others is actually a reflection of ourselves, so the great news here is that the reasons *why* you've picked your top five people are actually a reflection of the qualities you already possess or qualities you aspire to.

If you happened to have picked a couple of people for very similar reasons, say for example because they've demonstrated a huge amount of loyalty, then it's very likely this a quality that is very important to you – it is a standard you'd set for yourself and one that you would seek out in others.

"The older I get the less I listen to what people say and the more I look at what they do."

Andrew Carnegie, American industrialist

So take a moment to reflect back on the people you've chosen and, most importantly, the qualities you've identified in them, because these are *your* leadership qualities – they define the type of leader you are and the strengths that you can use to lead yourself and empower others.

Make it happen

Leaders by their very definition act differently from others. Apart from their inspiring qualities, what else makes someone a great leader?

One of their key characteristics is their instinct to take action. If they see an opportunity or indeed a problem they don't sit back and wait for others to do something – instead a leader will step forward on their own initiative and act. Leaders can be summarized as *people who create change*, things happen around them, they make a difference not only to their own lives but also to the lives of others. They *make* it happen.

Leaders are often born in a crisis and it's not until the need is there that they will find the courage and strength within themselves to step up and do the right thing. However that shouldn't mean that you need to wait until you find yourself in a crisis before you follow your leader instincts.

How many times have you found yourself in a situation when you were waiting or hoping someone else would take control, yet every instinct in *your* body was telling you something is not right?

If that ever happens then next time take the initiative – don't hesitate, instead act. You can choose to be a leader in *any* situation, no matter how trivial or small it may appear, and how you react could be a defining moment for you in your life. Trust your instincts, which are wired directly to your Scooby ears, and are usually 99.9 per cent accurate.

Stepping out of line

I was once checking in for a return charter flight having been on a group skiing holiday. On arrival at the airport everyone dutifully followed the signs to the allotted check-in desks where we waited with the 300 other passengers. *Two hours later* we were all still standing in line, waiting for the check-in desks to open but no staff had turned up. The display boards in the departure hall were still asking us to wait at the check-in area, yet the flight time gave no indication of a delay and time was fast ticking by. We were now less than 30 minutes away from the scheduled take-off time. The inbound flight had landed some time earlier – it all just didn't add up.

Every instinct in my body was telling me that somebody somewhere had made a big mistake and human error was to blame. We should have been checked in by now; yet everybody else was dutifully and unquestioningly waiting in line as per the instructions on the display boards, grumbling about the wait and how inefficient the airline was.

This situation was hardly life or death but clearly something was wrong and nobody appeared to be doing anything about it. I considered my options and decided to act.

Many of my friends discouraged me from doing anything, and wanted me to stay put like everyone else. On some level they probably felt uncomfortable with me stepping out of line but, as is often the case with those that love us, they were only trying to protect me, just in case I messed up and embarrassed myself. I just asked, 'What's the worst that could happen? I make an idiot out of myself – well, hey, I never take myself too seriously anyway, so I've got nothing to lose.'

As I didn't speak the local language I thought my best option was to make my way to the arrivals hall where hopefully the tour guide would now be collecting the inbound passengers and alert him to the problem. When I eventually located our representative he was astounded to hear that 300 people were still waiting to be checked in elsewhere in the airport, and that everyone had stood in a queue for two hours and not said anything!

Suddenly check-in staff came running from all directions and completed the fastest check-in I've ever experienced, checking in all 300 passengers in under 15 minutes! The entire plane-load of passengers was escorted through airport security to the awaiting aircraft, where everyone was boarded immediately and the plane miraculously left on time.

I found myself at the centre of everyone's attention, being slapped on the back and being praised for taking action. And I remember thinking how bizarre it all was and that all I had done was identify there was a problem and taken action to solve it. I only wish I had done so sooner, instead of waiting in line for two hours, which meant I'd missed the opportunity to go shopping in duty free.

Everybody else that day had the same opportunity, yet for two hours nobody took action. Everyone acknowledged that something was up and the situation didn't feel right, but perhaps due to their own lack of confidence or fear of looking foolish they chose to do nothing, waiting for someone else to take the lead. I'm not telling you this story because I believe I'm in any way better than anyone else, but I find it very interesting that the other 299 people that day were more concerned with staying in their own comfort zone rather than doing anything about an increasingly silly situation.

In Chapter 2 we discovered that our natural 'patterns' of behaviour often show up in lots of areas of our lives. If you had found yourself in the airport situation described above, what would you have done? If you think you would have waited for someone else to deal with the situation, then it's worthwhile asking yourself the question: why? Answering that question truthfully could be the key to unlocking your potential and taking your personal change to a whole new level. It's the real reason why you've previously held yourself back and stopped yourself from achieving.

What do you need to take action on in your life right now? It's time to step up and be the leader you were born to be. Take the initiative and take action. Do so without any expectation of reward or recognition from your peers and you will ultimately increase your influence over others. People will begin to look to you for answers and inspiration, viewing you as a role model. But remember, all leadership begins by influencing yourself first, then others around you.

Consistency and expectations

Another great behaviour all leaders demonstrate is their ability to be constant. There is nothing more unnerving than a leader who changes their mood or their mind as often as the wind blows. It's important that others who look up to you are able to predict the consequences of their own actions, i.e. they understand what is expected of them, what behaviour is acceptable and what behaviour carries consequences. They won't be focused on the task in hand if the whole time they are walking on egg shells wondering how their boss/spouse/parent is going to react today.

I've coached a couple of people through fairly negative work relationships, bordering on bullying by line managers, and the one thing in common in both these situations was the inconsistency of the managers, which left the people involved feeling completely inadequate and undervalued.

Decide what you need your colleagues, partner or family to do, then communicate with them your expectations, make your

ANOTHER GREAT BEHAVIOUR ALL LEADERS DEMONSTRATE IS THEIR ABILITY TO BE CONSTANT.

commitments clear and finally follow through. I stress this applies as much with your partner and family as in work. TV Supernanny Jo Frost is a big believer in consistency. If you set a child an expectation – say for example a bedtime routine that includes a bath, followed by a story, then an agreed time for bed – but only stick to it twice, the child's behaviour will deteriorate as they no longer understand what is acceptable and what isn't.

The same applies for everyone you deal with – you need to be consistent first, and then make sure you follow through once you've outlined your expectations for others.

If you must 'lose it' then make sure you do so well out of sight and sound of those you lead. Use your own peer group, not your team or children to blow off steam with; otherwise all you will do is undermine your own authority.

It's the small things that count

Making people feel valued is a huge part of being an inspiring leader. It's so simple to do in theory yet not always as easy to put into practice. It's always the tiny details that make a difference, but remembering to do them is the challenge.

Take time to say hello and goodbye to people. Be interested in them and really *hear* what they are saying. If it's personal, get it right. Things like spelling or pronouncing their name correctly are so important – getting this wrong is simply disrespectful and makes them feel that they are not important enough for you to get it right. Remember to say please and thank you. Be open and approachable and prepared to listen to other people's opinions. Be on time, as being late (particularly when it's a habit and not just because there was an accident on the motorway) simply sends a message that those waiting were not important enough to be on time for.

However, when I've asked people what is the one thing that makes a person feel most valued, it's simply doing what you say you will. There is nothing more frustrating for someone if you've made a commitment and then you break it seemingly flippantly. For example, if you've made a commitment to a team member to discuss their performance and then you cancel the meeting at short notice, that simply sends a message to that person they are not that important and whatever has replaced their meeting in your schedule is more important than their contribution. If you must change an appointment, give as much time as possible and communicate a clear reason why. The same goes for letting a friend down. And of course you can break a child's heart if you promise them something but then break the commitment because somebody or something else took priority. So stick to your commitments and make sure you follow them through.

If this is a challenge for you, you'd be better off taking on less commitments and managing other people's expectations at the outset, rather than saying yes to everyone and everything, just because you don't want to let anyone down – when in reality that's exactly what you'll end up doing. Instead recognize that it's your own desire to avoid rejection that's driving your need

STICK TO YOUR COMMITMENTS AND MAKE SURE YOU FOLLOW THEM THROUGH.

to say yes all the time, particularly when you know at the outset you've over-committed yourself.

Leaders are ultimately servers

I've yet to meet an effective leader who does not offer their service in some way. Great leaders have purpose, a goal which ultimately creates benefit for themselves as well as others – perhaps their family, their business and their customers, their community or, on an even larger scale, society in general.

Of course, there will also be people in positions of authority who do not follow this trend. They may have other motives for creating success through their leadership. Perhaps their intentions initially were pure but changed once they achieved their success. These people may be remembered but perhaps not always for all the right reasons. Don't fall into that trap.

The people who acquire the greatest levels of respect from others do so usually because they are motivated by their desire to serve.

I'm very fortunate to be born into a family with a strong leadership legacy. My grandfather, Siddle C. Cook, was an extremely successful businessman who came from a humble background and went on to build a number of very successful companies in a variety of industries during his lifetime.

As a young girl I was hugely inspired by my Granddad, not just because he was my grandfather and I loved him dearly, but from a very early age I was aware of the amount of respect he commanded from everyone who knew him. I never heard him raise his voice, yet people stopped and listened to what he had to say. Although he was clearly a successful man himself, I never heard him brag or attribute his success to his efforts alone; it was always about a team effort and a lot of hard work.

I loved the fact that his success had clearly not changed him as a person. Even though his success meant that he could live in a slightly bigger house, and take nicer holidays with his family, he was famous for driving his Mercedes Benz most days wearing a pair of oily workman's overalls, rigger boots and a flat cap. That's the person he was before he became successful and the person he remained after he created his business success.

I remember when he died the hundreds of letters and cards our family received, not only offering their condolences but also containing stories about how he had helped them or offered his advice. I remember reading a letter from one man who recounted how 30 years earlier when he had been a young man himself with an ambition to set up his own photography business he had approached my grandfather. Granddad had not only given him the money to buy his equipment – not loaned him the money, just gave him the investment – but had been very generous with his advice and mentorship. No one in our family had ever heard of this man or had any knowledge of Granddad's actions. Clearly Granddad had not wanted, or indeed needed, any acknowledgement for his actions; he simply did what he believed to be right, without any expectation of reward. What an inspiration!

However, today I'm also inspired by my cousin Nigel, who is now managing director of a large haulage company which my grandfather and uncle started in the 1970s. I recently interviewed Nigel at a local conference, asking him about his journey in business, what he has learned and his ambitions for the future. I might just add how uncomfortable he felt about accepting the invitation to speak at this event and how much I had to persuade him to talk publicly about his success. It was his response to one of my questions that struck a particular chord. I'd asked him what gets him out of bed in the morning, especially when times are tough and business isn't going well. He responded, 'The way I look at it, there are 350 families depending on me, 350 mortgages that need to be paid every month, including my own. If I don't do my job, how can I expect anyone else to do theirs?' Another example of a great leader who is also a great server.

In order to be an inspiring leader, be very clear about your intentions. If you desire greatness in any area of your life, it is absolutely acceptable (in fact a prerequisite) to want to achieve your own goals, including materialistic success if that's what you desire, but why not use that ambition to positively affect the lives of others around you as well? We all have the potential to be an inspiring leader, and to make a positive difference to the lives of others.

SUMMARY

- Leaders are called inspiring because of the type of person they are and the way that they lead rather than for what they've achieved.

- Leadership has nothing to do with a job title or responsibilities given by another. A person may have no formal responsibilities yet be an inspiring leader to others.

- Leaders ultimately create change.

- Take action. Use your initiative to step out from the crowd and make change happen.

- Be consistent and make others feel valued.

- Great leaders serve a purpose that is more than just their personal gain and do so without any expectation of reward.

12

**Be fit for your life –
the power of boundless energy**

How you feel, physically and mentally, has a huge impact on living a more fulfilled, happier life. There's very little point in making big, wonderful changes and having a bright future ahead if you have no life in your body to enjoy it! The New You needs a healthy body.

So many people take their physical body for granted. They expect it to work every day and do very little to support it, then become dumbfounded when illness strikes them down, seemingly unexpectedly from nowhere. In fact the lifestyle choices they have been making for years have slowly eroded their health.

The body you've got is the only one you're going to get. It's not like the family car, which you can use and abuse until it wears out, then pop to your local garage and trade it in for a newer, shinier model – this is it! So you need to know how to get the best from it.

What is health?

The first World Health Assembly in 1948 defined health as:

> *'A state of complete physical, mental and social well-being and not merely the absence of disease or infirmity.'*

A complete state of physical, mental and social well-being – a mind and body that is in complete balance and working at its optimum.

Health has nothing to do with body weight. Yes, being underweight or overweight is a symptom of poor health and a warning sign that something is out of balance. But likewise it is possible to appear to be very fit and healthy yet not be truly healthy at all.

You know what healthy feels like, just as you know how unhealthy feels. Remember that unhealthy is not when you are

YOU KNOW WHAT HEALTHY FEELS LIKE, JUST AS YOU KNOW HOW UNHEALTHY FEELS.

laid up in bed with the flu; unhealthy is the state that most of us live our lives, because we don't place *building health* high enough on our agenda for life.

What does healthy feel like for you?

I gave up measuring my own health by the dial on the bathroom scales a long time ago. Instead I measure my own health by how much *energy* I have to do the things I want to do.

Over the years I've taken my own body for granted a few times and, boy, have I paid the price. I've been guilty of eating and drinking the wrong things, I've stayed up late too often, I've worked too hard, I've worried too much, I've over-exercised, I've not exercised enough, I've been overweight and dangerously underweight at different times of my life. What I do recognize now is that all these actions were my own choices and with every choice comes consequences, an outcome. And if you don't like the outcome then remember: change the behaviour. Now I take full responsibility for my health and wellbeing. If I'm feeling unhealthy I realize it's because of things I've been doing or *not* doing.

Think of your body as a glass tumbler. Within the glass is some dirty water, which represents the toxicity within your body. The natural level of the water line represents the natural level of toxicity within your body.

Everybody's natural toxicity level is different so the first step in building more energy in your life is to understand that your constitution and what it can deal with is likely to be very different from somebody else's. Our body is constantly aiming to create more health by performing one key function – *cleansing our system of toxins* and therefore lowering the level of the water line in the glass.

Examples of the way toxins enter our body

- Polluted air.

- Unpurified water.

- Pesticides on food and additives in food.

- Natural acids that form in some foods, such as red meat.

- Any drink that contains sugar, caffeine or artificial flavourings.

- Any non-natural substances that we place on our skin or bodies which are absorbed, such as deodorant or toothpaste.

- Smoking.

- Lactic acid that builds up in our muscles after vigorous exercise.

- Negative emotions that cause hormonal changes, such as a stress response, which can build up toxins in the tissues.

- Some medications – even though in some cases they may be necessary they are still toxic, which is why they have side-effects.

However, our bodies are also being bombarded with toxins from everywhere within our environment, adding toxins into our system which metaphorically speaking raises the level of the water line in the glass tumbler. The higher the level of toxins in your body, the less well you will feel. Toxins are present everywhere and some we simply cannot avoid, but many toxins that enter our system are self-imposed through our lifestyle choices – and these are the ones that we can have some control over.

If we absorb toxins and cleanse them from our system at the same rate, then the level of the water in the glass stays the same, so our health neither improves nor deteriorates. If our bodies cleanse more toxins from our systems at a faster rate than we absorb them then obviously the level of the water in the tumbler would drop, representing a cleaner system and a higher level of health and energy.

Likewise, if we load our system with more toxins than we are able to clear, then the level of the water line rises, representing a more toxic body and a lower level of health. The faster we load toxins, the greater the immediate impact on our wellbeing.

Ever wondered why you have a hangover after a heavy night out drinking lots of alcohol, eating a dodgy kebab and getting only a few hours' sleep? It's no surprise really, when you consider the heavy load of toxins you've just placed in your body. However, the overloading of toxins on our body can often be very, very gradual and one that we tend to ignore, blaming any symptoms we may experience on our current levels of overwork, emotional stress or, most commonly, 'getting older' – and we accept these as a fact of life.

When you consider the 'toxic' list from the previous page, clearly there are some things that we can have more influence over than others. For example, it would be unrealistic to carry around your own supply of purified air, but it is realistic to change your habits to reduce the toxicity you absorb from other areas in your life.

I was a heavy social drinker in my 20s. I never had a drinking problem, but like many people of my generation I used to go out every weekend with friends to drink and party until the wee hours. Not in itself a problem, but added to that I also had a very stressful job and worked very long hours, and although I believed that the drinking and partying was helping me unwind, in fact it was having the opposite effect on my health.

Initially my symptoms were quite subtle. I started getting sore throats, followed by colds that never seemed to go away, followed by spots on my face, followed by pain in my leg muscles and lymph nodes, followed by night sweats and leg cramps, followed by insomnia and poor appetite. I kept on ignoring the build-up of symptoms until one day I physically collapsed and then basically had to stay in bed for six months. That got my attention! When I realized that I didn't have a specific illness that a magic pill could cure and I had simply eroded my health over time, only then did I choose to do something about my health and energy levels. It had taken me about six years to erode my health and it took about the same amount of time to build my health back up.

Now I listen to my body and I'm aware when the water line is starting to rise and the levels of toxicity are on the up. So, in my case, the minute I get a sore throat, that's it. Alarm bells are ringing and I do something immediately to help boost my immune system and enable my body to cleanse out some toxins, while also making a conscious effort to reduce my toxin intake.

Here are some examples of poor health and optimum health symptoms that occur long before the universe comes along and gives you a proper whack! with its big disease baseball bat and you wake up one day with diabetes, heart disease or something even worse.

Symptoms of poor health	Symptoms of optimum health
Low energy	Boundless energy
Wake up feeling tired	Wake up feeling alive
Poor appetite	Healthy appetite
Unhealthy weight or rapid weight change	Healthy stable weight
Low or no sex drive	Can't get enough!
Apathy for life	Passion for life
Erratic mood swings	Emotional control
Spots or skin problems	Glowing, radiant skin
Hair loss (not related to baldness in men)	Strong shiny hair and nails
The 'whites' of the eyes are discoloured, often yellow	Sparkling white eyes
Furry tongue or bad breath	Clean tasting palate
Dark, strong-smelling urine	Pale, straw-coloured, odourless urine
Muscle pain or tension in the body	Strong healthy body which moves easily
Low immune system resulting in lots of viral infections	Strong immune system, no viral infections
Digestive problems (you know, the things we don't like to talk about at the dinner table!)	Good digestion and transit time (the time it takes for food to go from one end to the other – a healthy system will eliminate waste within 12–24 hours)

So what happens if the levels of toxicity in your body keep rising? Think back to the metaphor of a glass of dirty water: what would happen if you keep pouring dirty water into the tumbler? Eventually the glass would be unable to hold the increased water content and the water would overflow.

When this happens in your body, it means that your system is now unable to cleanse toxins as quickly as they are building up in your body and you are now at risk of disease. At the very least, you're more likely to succumb to one of the many germs and viruses that we're all exposed to in daily human contact – usually a cold or flu.

Treat the symptoms, find the cause

When you begin to feel unwell, how do you normally react? Do you take a pill or potion to fix you up, or would you also think about what might be the underlying cause and take preventative action to reduce the toxic load on your system to support your immune function? It's not an either/or question. Ideally you can do both.

My friend Neal has a great metaphor that illustrates this point. Imagine you are driving your car down the road and suddenly a warning light flashes on the dashboard. So you pull over but instead of investigating further you simply pull out the corresponding wire so that the light stops flashing. Problem solved, but is it really? The light has stopped flashing, the warning signal or the symptom has been fixed, but the reason for it flashing in the first place still remains.

If you have a headache, then by all means take a pain killer – you don't need to suffer unnecessary pain in this day and age – but also ask yourself *why* you've got that headache. The pain is merely a symptom of something which is out of balance in your body: perhaps you are dehydrated, perhaps you are tired, perhaps you are emotionally out of balance. If the headache reoccurs and persists then it may be an indication of something deeper that would need the investigation of a doctor. But it's also worth considering some of the available alternative therapies which aim to restore balance at a deeper emotional, physical and spiritual level.

Doing what you know you should

Your health is one of the areas in your life where, if you are not doing what you know you should, then it'll show up. It will be evident all over your body and you can't hide from it. You and eventually everyone will be able to see it. Most of us know what we should be doing: eat more good stuff, eat less bad stuff, drink more water and excercise sensibly and regularly – not a great shock to anyone. So if we already know all of this then why do many of us fail to consistently stick with it?

The answer again lies in your driving emotions and your desires to move away from pain and move closer to pleasure. Many people get an emotional pay-off when they eat (or in some cases don't eat) or when they exercise (or again don't exercise). If you feel some form of pleasure, perhaps a feeling of being naughty or perhaps a feeling of control when you eat a chocolate muffin, then this is an example where you are using food as a way of making yourself feel better. So, if this isn't good for you long term, then what should you do?

IT MAKES NO SENSE TO STRAP YOURSELF IN FOR A WHITE-KNUCKLE RIDE BY GOING ON A CRASH DIET.

In order to develop a healthy lifestyle, it makes no sense to strap yourself in for a white-knuckle ride by going on a crash diet or a mad exercise regime which is only a short-term fix – you are only setting yourself up for a fall. (Just like the rocket taking off into space and eventually falling back to earth with empty fuel tanks.) Instead you first need to associate more pain with being unhealthy and treating your body badly, and more pleasure with making wise, healthy choices.

So instead of feeling pleasure when you eat that chocolate muffin, consider the impact it will have on your health. Choose to feel proud and good about yourself when you choose to eat a more healthy alternative. If you feel tempted to make a less healthy choice, picture in your mind how it feels to be unhealthy, as ultimately that is what will happen if you continue to make poor choices.

The second step is to follow one of the overall philosophies of this book and make smaller shifts which you can sustain over time. It may take longer to achieve your health goals, but you will achieve your goals in a much more sustainable way.

If you want to lose 10 kilos in weight you could do it in a day – by chopping your right leg off! Not an option most people would choose. However if you just made small shifts in your daily choices it's feasible to lose half a kilo a week. In only 20 weeks you will have achieved the same goal, yet you get to keep your right leg – bonus!

Rebuild your health from the inside out

Any medical practitioner, traditional or alternative, will tell you that all health begins from the inside out, from a cellular level within your body. You can mask poor health with medication, make-up or cosmetic treatments, but nothing you apply to your skin or take internally will cover indefinitely poor health from within.

When you are looking to build your health from the inside out there are three things to consider.

1 Fuel for health

What fuel do you put in your car? What fuel do the Formula 1 teams put in their racing cars? The higher the performance required of the car, the higher the grade of the fuel. You wouldn't put vegetable oil in a Formula 1 car and expect to win the race.

So what fuel do you put in your personal racing car? I'm not advocating you become an organic vegan – I'm not one personally. I eat good stuff and sometimes less good stuff. I don't believe you should never have a glass of wine or a bar of chocolate, should you choose, but what I do recommend is that you work out what works for your body and pay attention to how it feels when you eat well and stay well hydrated, as opposed to have a few days where your diet is less balanced. What impact do the changes in your diet have on your energy levels? I'm confident that when you support your system with good-quality fuel you will be rewarded with good-quality health and higher levels of energy.

Stick to the basic principles of:

- eat 5 portions of fruit and veg a day
- drink 2 litres of water a day
- exercise sensibly 3 times a week.

Get to know your body, reduce your toxin intake and you won't go far wrong.

2 Physical health

Your body is made up of millions of cells that are organized in the most efficient way to allow you to move and function in life. The two keys that affect the effectiveness of your physical health are your internal bio-chemistry and your structural system.

Your bio-chemistry is affected obviously by the fuel you put into your body. If your diet is deficient in particular nutrients then over time this will take its toll on your health. Your emotions, which we deal with in the next section, also have a massive impact on your bio-chemistry.

However, the effectiveness of your structural system will also have an impact on your health. Obviously if you sensibly exercise your physical body and, as a result, it is strong and supple, your physical health will benefit. However, many people are unaware of the impact of their lifestyles on their physical body and the impact that that has on their health and energy levels.

Modern life creates stress and tension on our physical bodies that pull them out of their natural alignment, and usually we are unaware that this is even happening, unless we have it corrected.

A body in pure structural alignment is one that can work at its optimum. My friend Dr Fiona Ellis, who specialises in osteopathy, describes your spine as being the motorway of your body. Everything in your body flows through your spine: your circulatory system, your lymph system and most importantly your nervous system. If your alignment is out of balance then imagine the impact on a motorway if two out of three lanes are closed. The traffic backs up, diversions are put in place and long delays occur, which is exactly what happens in your body – it works less efficiently. Other areas then have to compensate and pick up the slack.

I first went to see Fiona about 10 years ago with a pain in my left shoulder. I was amazed when she started working on my right knee. I said, 'Hang on a minute, the pain is here', and she responded, 'Ah yes, but the problem is here!'

It's fairly likely that unless you are already doing something about your physical health, your body will be out of balance. You can help yourself enormously by keeping your physical body strong and supple and by building stretching into your routine.

Yoga and Pilates are both great at supporting these principles. Take time out to enjoy a massage, which helps to release lactic acid build up in your soft tissues. I also strongly advocate regular visits to the osteopath or chiropractor, not to treat chronic problems but as a preventative health-boosting measure. You don't wait until your teeth are rotten and falling out before you go to the dentist and maintaining a healthy spine is just as important.

3 Emotional health

The final element – and equally important to a fit body – is to ensure you have optimum emotional health. This once again brings us full circle to the importance of maintaining a healthy psychology – and you will appreciate from Part 1 of this book how much of this is within your own control.

In order for you to 'feel' a certain way your brain has to change the bio-chemistry of your body by changing the hormonal levels in your blood. In its simplest form, good feelings help build health; negative feelings reduce health.

If you've ever watched the Robin Williams film *Patch Adams*, based on the life of Hunter 'Patch' Adams, an American medical doctor who believes strongly that laughter is the best medicine, then you will appreciate the importance of a positive mindset in the healing process and the maintenance of long-term health.

We often label any emotional imbalances as simply being 'stressed', but stress is only a word used to describe a body that

STRESS IS ONLY A WORD USED TO DESCRIBE A BODY THAT IS OUT OF BALANCE.

is out of balance, and we've already covered the impacts on your health when that happens. Therefore, you now also have another reason to master your emotions and continue to maintain healthy emotional choices, as ultimately they also affect your health and energy levels.

Easy strategies to build long-term health

Health is a lifestyle choice, so the best way to maintain optimum health is to find the small, simple ways to make positive changes in your daily routine that support a healthy mind, body and immune system over the long term. If you have a blow-out one day, don't panic – simply make better choices the next day to create a positive counter-balance.

Building long-term health

- Aim to eat your five portions a day.

- Buy a juicer or blender and make a home-made juice or smoothie (preferably green in colour) to add to your daily diet.

- Eat as much food in its raw, unprocessed state as possible. Instead of snacking on crisps or chocolates, choose snacks of carrots, apples, bananas, nuts or whatever takes your fancy. The more natural, the better.

- Eat consciously, making sure you chew your food well.

- Reduce, or better still cut out, *bad* drinks and replace with filtered water.

- Drink caffeine in moderation and preferably replace with herbal alternatives.

- Practise 10–20 minutes of meditation and positive visualization every day (twice a day preferably) to support your emotional well-being.

- Have great sex! The feel-good hormones released in an orgasm do wonders for your health.

- Go to bed at the same time every night and sleep for the same amount each night. Aim to get to bed a minimum of an hour before midnight, which helps your body regulate your natural bio-rhythms.

- Get on the floor and stretch your body out.

- Exercise sensibly on a regular basis to improve your aerobic fitness levels.

- Get a massage.

- Go for a colonic irrigation, if that appeals.

- Use a nose bidet to flush out your sinuses, using warm, slightly salted water.

- Jump on a rebounder for five minutes to get the lymph moving through your body.

- Have a regular spinal adjustment for optimum spinal health.

- If you have an ongoing imbalance which traditional medicine has not been able to resolve long term, invest in a visit to a naturopath or any of the alternative therapists to help uncover any other underlying problems. (Remember to always make sure you visit a licensed practitioner.)

If you implement only five of the changes from the list above, in a very short period of time, usually days, you will see an improvement in your health; implement more and your health and energy will radically improve.

Remember, it's OK to have a day off every now and then and indulge yourself in a glass of wine or a heavy meal: it is all about balance. The most important thing is to become in tune and then act on what your body needs to give you the energy you desire to live your life to the fullest.

SUMMARY

- Health is not just the absence of disease but the balance of mind, body and spirit.

- Measure your own health by your levels of energy.

- Learn what healthy feels like in your body and what affects your levels of energy.

- Use traditional medicine to treat symptoms; use holistic medicine to uncover and then correct deeper imbalances.

- Build health from the inside out by taking responsibility for:
  - fuel for health
  - physical health
  - emotional health.

- Your health is ultimately your choice, but don't panic if you lose the plot one day – just counter-balance poor choices with better choices the next day.

13

Make it stick –
the power of creating
'New You' habits

One of the themes running through this book is the idea that small, consistent changes create long-term success.

I have client who initially signed up for a 12-month coaching programme, but after attending 1 of our 3-day training programmes, called me the next day to say how much he had enjoyed the 3 days and didn't feel that he needed to continue his personal coaching programme. He felt that he really now knew what he should be doing with his life and just simply needed to get on with it.

I applauded him for his enthusiasm and his new levels of confidence and self-belief and encouraged him wholeheartedly to take the actions he had committed to. However, I reminded him that the reason he had selected the 12-month coaching programme initially was that he had wanted some ongoing support as he acknowledged that he had had similar experiences at various times of his life, yet failed to sustain the changes over the long term.

Less than four weeks later, I received the call to say that he had lost his momentum and his confidence had evaporated into thin air. This is not usual, as it's natural to go through a process of levelling following a huge emotional high. When we met up we looked at his daily habits to establish where he was going off track and together came up with an achievable, sustainable plan that he could use on a day-to-day basis.

"The secret is not in the knowing, but in the doing."

Michael Heppell, author and international motivational speaker

So how do you do it? There are three methods to create sustainable change in your life and this final chapter is going to give you the multiple strategies that you need to ensure you consistently act on the decisions you've now made.

Creating sustainable change

The three strategies that when applied together create massive momentum are:

1 Ongoing stimuli.

2 A supportive environment.

3 Powerful peers.

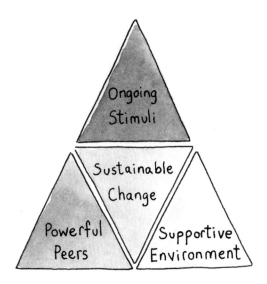

So let's take each of these individually and decide how you can make smaller changes from each area to add into your everyday life. Many of the techniques I suggest here overlap with others, but we will go through them individually.

1 Ongoing stimuli

Success doesn't just reward the people who know what they want, it is created by those who continue to take action to get it. Therefore, in order to maintain your momentum, stop focusing on how much you know, instead focus on how much you are doing.

So, if you want to stay physically fit and toned you go and work out regularly in the gym – you have your routine, so many minutes of cardio followed by a routine of lifting weights. If you miss a session the effects won't be too catastrophic immediately, but miss a couple of weeks and you will feel the effects on your body.

It's important to maintain positive empowering stimuli as you continue to grow and learn every day on your journey through life. What works for you today may not work tomorrow, as life changes and moves on around you, and you need to be able to continue to grow and adapt to the challenges that life presents.

Your mind is like a sponge and is soaking up everything it is exposed to, be that positive or negative stimuli. Therefore it makes sense to keep feeding it with positive stimuli to keep yourself motivated.

Negativity is everywhere – even though you may not be aware of it. Nobody is completely immune, so make sure you choose to surround yourself with empowering positive stimuli rather than stimuli that will automatically drain your positive mental

YOU NEED TO BE ABLE TO CONTINUE TO GROW AND ADAPT TO THE CHALLENGES THAT LIFE PRESENTS.

attitude, your energy and your motivation in an instant – if you let it.

Here are some examples of ongoing stimuli that you can use to build positivity into your daily life.

Keep reading

What was the last book you read, other than this one of course? Continue to read empowering, uplifting material to learn from but also to keep your mind in tip-top condition.

Someone once said to me, 'Why on earth would you want to go through life and make all your own mistakes just so that you can learn from them?' Many famous people have documented their own mistakes, so get reading, learn from their mistakes and avoid making them for yourself!

As you're reading something, don't focus on how much you already know, which if you are well read in a particular subject is highly likely. Instead focus on what you can apply positively in your life to make the changes you desire.

Go on courses

Live courses and training programmes are a great form of positive stimulus, if of course they are good quality and delivered in the right way. In order to participate, you have to remove yourself from your day-to-day life for a short period of time, and put yourself in a controlled environment with no distractions and with a similar group of peers who are also going through the same experience. If you can invest the time and money, live courses are a great way to improve your skills very quickly.

Audio training programmes allow you to listen in the car or on your MP3 player and are a great way to learn some new ideas, refresh learning from the past and maintain an ongoing positive stimulus. There are hundreds of audio programmes available so choose one that is right for you. However, if listening to audio programmes is not your thing (especially if you have a preferred visual style like me), then get hold of some DVD training programmes. Personally, I can watch a video for 4 hours straight and learn so much, yet struggle to listen to 30 minutes of an audio training programme: I need the visual references. Either way, find what works for you – then use it.

You could also try a virtual training environment where through the guidance of a trainer a group of people can be trained simultaneously online – without you ever having to leave your desk! Just find the medium that suits you the best and then continue to immerse yourself in it.

Use technology

Most of us are surrounded by technology, all day every day, so why not use it as a way of triggering ongoing stimuli? For example, subscribe to a quote of the day email or text messaging service.

Or why not put a motivational message, perhaps one of your mantras, on your screen saver that intermittently pops up on your computer?

TV and film

A recent study by Childwise, a UK charity, found that the average family in the UK spends over five hours a day in front of the box: so monitor what you watch.

Your brain is like a huge sponge and is unconsciously soaking up information all the time, whether you are aware of it or not. And many TV programmes and films that we could allow ourselves to be exposed to are primarily negative.

I don't believe the reverse psychology of 'I love watching people who have miserable lives, because it makes my life look rosy!' Rubbish. Whatever you expose your mind to, you unconsciously absorb and it's emotionally conditioning your psyche. So switch off the programmes that are designed to basically show other people's misery, be it fictional or factual.

Don't spend all day watching the news. Do watch the headlines so that you are in touch with what is going on in the world, but be wary of deeply immersing yourself in other people's negativity. Instead find programmes and films that are uplifting, and spend time being entertained by positive influences.

Creative visualization

We've covered the importance of practising visualization earlier, so make sure you make time every day to visualize your goals, remembering to emotionally associate with achieving your desired outcomes. I would suggest you place visualization up there with 'breathing' on the scale of importance in sustaining the New You. Make it part of your daily routine – set your alarm 10 minutes earlier if you have to and do it before you start your day, or do it whilst you exercise or lying in a relaxing bath. Alternatively stop the car on your journey home and spend 10 minutes refocusing your mind with visualizing your goals and dreams.

I do my visualizing every morning in the shower (it's about the only time I get to myself). When and where you do it is less important than making sure you do it daily, ideally twice a day. I guarantee the more you associate with your wish list the faster you will attract the resources and energy you need to create your goals.

Mantras

In Chapter 5 on managing your self-talk we introduced *mantras* as a way of conditioning your internal voice. So if you haven't done so already, saying your mantras every day is a simple and easy way to continue to condition yourself on a daily basis.

Again I make time to say mine in the shower (sometimes I even get washed!). Another popular place is in the car, particularly if you need to gain control of your emotions quickly, for example before an important meeting.

Use your mantras on an ongoing basis to condition yourself, as well as anywhere and anytime you need to change your mindset quickly.

Bounce like a Tigger

Chapter 12 dealt with multiple strategies to build your health and energy, and this also needs to become part of your daily routine, just as you clean your teeth and wash every day without even thinking about it. So if you haven't already, pick the areas from the list on pages 202–3 that you are going to implement and start now!

We have a rebounder in our office which is a great tool to build energy if our energy levels have dropped throughout the day for any reason. It's great to see people in the middle of the afternoon taking a couple of minutes out to have a brief bounce, especially if they need to rebuild their positive emotional states. Everyone can bounce like a Tigger for a few moments every day.

If bouncing's not your thing, you could instead go for a 15-minute walk at lunchtime to rejuvenate and refresh your mind and body. The point is making the decision to move and then acting on it.

A supportive environment

As well as maintaining ongoing positive stimuli in your routine, it's really important to *set up* your environment in the most positive way possible. Your behaviour is hugely influenced by your environment. If you remember from Part 1 of this book, your entire life experience has been shaped by your environmental experiences and how you've responded to them. Therefore, it's important to ensure your environment from now on is designed to support the New You.

> "If you put good people in bad systems you get bad results. You have to water the flowers you want to grow."
>
> Stephen Covey, American writer

If you've ever had the pleasure of visiting a Walt Disney World theme park, you will know the impact it can have on your mood. People can be arguing in the car park, yet the moment everyone is inside the Magic Kingdom they transform into nicer citizens, smiling at strangers, picking up the tiniest piece of litter and are quite happy to wait in a queue for hours on end for their favourite ride, such is the power of the environment. Likewise, a different type of environment can draw out a different type of behaviour in a person. I arrived at King's Cross Station in London recently and as I descended the steps into the tube station I accidentally brushed past a fellow commuter. I found myself automatically smiling at the stranger and making an apology, only to be met with a glazed stare in response. What was really interesting is that it only took a further few seconds for my mood to be dragged down by the environment. What would have been my normal, positive response in my usual environment had now had to become a more conscious choice in this less supportive environment.

I've seen it happen following a training programme where someone, or indeed a group of people, has made empowering decisions and is all fired up, only to return to their normal environment where their behaviour slips back within a matter of days. Therefore, it's important to ensure that you plaster your environment with emotional reminders that 'trigger' your positive behaviour on an ongoing basis.

Make your goals visual

One of the most important tasks that you *must* do is to take your wish list and create a visual representation of your goals. Take a really big piece of card and gather pictures and photographs that represent your goals and dreams. Build it into a collage and then place this *goalboard* somewhere where you see it every day.

If there is a particular car or house you want, take a test drive or view the house, then take its picture (preferably with you in it) and place it on your goalboard. Every day as you visualize, imagine yourself living in that house, or owning that car. At the very least place a picture on your fridge!

In order to create a balanced life your goalboard should include visual representations of every part of your life that you wish to create – yourself, your relationships, your finances, your health, places you would like to visit and your dreams and aspirations for your work and anything else you want.

If you are responsible for your work environment, get your company's, or your team's, goals on the walls. When you go into a classroom at school, look how many colourful pictures are used to stimulate the children. I'm not suggesting that you turn your workplace into a kindergarten, but making sure you have your targets and successes visible is very effective as it keeps everyone focused on a day-to-day basis and at the same time creates *belief* that the outcomes will and can be achieved.

Music

Just as when we were discussing the importance of watching empowering TV programmes and films, listening to uplifting music is another great way of building triggers into your environment. We all process music at a deeper level in our mind and the right music can change our mood very, very quickly. Think about it. If you go to a party and the DJ is rubbish, what's the impact on the party atmosphere? Yet a brilliant party that you remember for the rest of your life is usually triggered by a great atmosphere, which normally includes a great DJ, who plays the best music.

We can easily use music to create what is known as an *anchor* to unconsciously trigger a positive mood in ourselves. The way to create an anchor is to play a particular piece of music when you feel a certain way. For example, I have a particular track that I play when I feel really, really positive. Then on a day when I don't feel quite so happy, I play that track and my brain remembers the way it makes me feel, and my mood instantly lifts. It's the same principle that happens when you hear the music that was played when you were on holiday and suddenly you're instantly transported back to that moment

Plan your success

Have you ever been on a training programme, perhaps through work, and you feel all fired up, then when you go back to work you are frustrated that the systems and processes are not set up to support the New You? And before you know it you give up, because what's the point? Instead, you need to make your systems work for you and that includes making your plan for success.

Take your goals from your wish list and compile an action plan with some interim milestones that you can use to measure your success. The bigger the goal, the more you may need to chunk it down into smaller, achievable targets.

For example, if you have a goal to radically change your financial circumstances, it's likely that you may need to take lots of smaller actions. So, for example:

- read a personal finance book or go on a course to skill-up in some key areas
- manage your debt in the most cost-effective way by transferring all loans to the best possible deals on the marketplace
- draw up your life budget and decide how much you will allow yourself in various areas of your life, then review your progress weekly
- decide how much you will save every month and track your progress
- look for creative ways to increase your income
- clear all clutter from your life by selling or giving away what you don't need
- decide on a long-term investment plan and start straight away with small, efficient investments.

Sometimes we can be overwhelmed if our goals appear so far away from our current starting point. That's when it's really important to chunk them down and build a clear action plan with time scales that may still be stretching but at least you know you can achieve.

I use what I call the *traffic light* system to set and track my plans. I do this for the business, with everyone in the team, and even with my husband for our family goals. Take a piece of plain paper and draw two lines down it to make three columns, and write red, amber and green at the top of each of the columns. Basically, just like a real set of traffic lights, this system has three categories.

- Green means *actions from now!* These are all the commitments you start on now and are simply changes in your behaviour that you make a commitment to do from now on.

- Amber means *30-day goal* and signifies the outcomes you want to achieve in the next 30 days.

- Red represents your *3-month goal*.

An example for someone who has a particular weight-related goal is shown here:

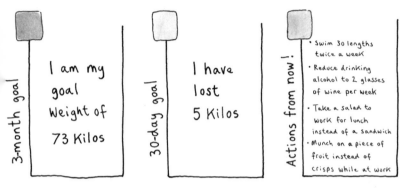

3-month goal
I am my goal weight of 73 Kilos

30-day goal
I have lost 5 Kilos

Actions from now!
- Swim 30 lengths twice a week
- Reduce drinking alcohol to 2 glasses of wine per week
- Take a salad to work for lunch instead of a sandwich
- Munch on a piece of fruit instead of crisps while at work

The whole purpose of using the traffic light system is to maintain your focus. It's so easy to be determined to achieve your goal at the moment you make the decision, yet very often your determination drifts if you don't maintain your focus.

So take your wish list and break it down. What goals can you achieve in the next three months (moving you in the direction you wish to go in)? Then break those goals down into monthly outcomes, and then daily and weekly actions. Once you have a plan, it's simply a process of following it.

Repeat this process for every goal on your wish list and keep it with you every day. Just knowing you have created your plan and it is close to you will unconsciously keep you focused on it.

I plan my week ahead every Sunday evening – it's a habit I've developed over the years. I spend around 90 minutes every Sunday night, looking through my diary for the following week, firing off emails and checking my traffic lights to see if there are any major commitments I need to focus on that week or self-imposed deadlines approaching.

If I don't do this, my week usually descends into unstructured chaos and I end up running around like a headless chicken. Whereas the weeks when I have planned ahead, I'm much more mentally focused and everything in my life runs much more smoothly.

Find a diary system and stick to it

I don't believe it works to have one diary for work and one for home: keep all dates in the same system. It doesn't matter whether it is a paper or an electronic diary – find one you are comfortable with and keep it simple.

Create a reward system

It's really important to remember to enjoy the fruits of your labour! Sometimes we become so focused on achieving our next goal that we forget to celebrate the successes we have achieved!

Take a holiday and spend some of the money you've worked so hard to make. Plan time in your schedule to spend with the people who are most important to you and share your success and rewards with them.

However, you can also use a reward system on a daily basis to keep you motivated on the actions you've committed to. These rewards don't need to be big ones. Deciding to stop and have a cup of tea when you've completed a piece of work or the

REMEMBER TO ENJOY THE FRUITS OF YOUR LABOUR!

promise of a relaxing bath when you've finished something can be sufficient to keep you motivated. Obviously this only works if you are disciplined in your approach.

Powerful peers

This is the final element to incorporate into your life to ensure that you sustain the changes for the New You. Research has shown that we are likely to conform to the standards of our peer group and we become most like the five people we spend the most time with. A peer can be a member of your family, a friend, someone you work with, a mentor or boss, or in fact anyone you have in your life. However, the role of a true powerful peer is quite specific.

The role of a powerful peer

- Believes in you unconditionally.
- Does not disempower you or put you down.
- Supports your goals and dreams.
- Reminds you that when things don't go your way it's just another opportunity to learn from your experiences.
- Holds you to a higher standard.
- Makes you accountable for your successes and your failures.
- Encourages you to stick to your commitments.
- Is pleased for you when you create success, as opposed to being jealous of it.

Look at the list above, and then look at the people you spend the most time with. Do they do any of the things on the list? It's interesting when you start to think about this, particularly with your family. I'm not suggesting that you stop spending time with your family members just because they don't fulfil your criteria of a powerful peer. However it's interesting that they are often the people we do spend a lot of time with, yet for various reasons are not always the most supportive. Usually this isn't on purpose, but often as a method of protecting us from ourselves – perhaps they would rather we didn't go out into the world and achieve our dreams, particularly if our aspirations are greater than the definition of success they have for their lives.

When I started my business I made a conscious effort to go out and find other people in business who would encourage and support me when things were tough. So I joined a number of professional business organizations, which initially was daunting, but I found people were very generous with their support and encouragement.

How do you find powerful peers?

The first obvious area is to look at your current network of friends, family and colleagues. Among them there will be people who fulfil the role of a powerful peer – find ways to spend more time with them. Remember one of the rules in connecting with people is to be interested rather than interesting.

ONE OF THE RULES IN CONNECTING WITH PEOPLE IS TO BE INTERESTED RATHER THAN INTERESTING.

The other simple way is to seek out and then join either professional or social networks where you are likely to meet the kind of people who you need to surround yourself with. There will be plenty in your area, you just need to do your research.

I would suggest that you ensure the culture of the group is action-orientated, has strong leadership and a strong purpose that fits your objectives, be that raising money for charity, learning something together, building your respective businesses, or simply socializing and having fun.

The other way you can use a power peer to support you is to find a professional mentor or coach. There are charitable organizations that will find you a mentor who has been there and got the T-shirt, someone who can give you the benefit of their experience; alternatively choose to invest in a professional coach.

When you are paying someone to effectively be your peer, they have a vested interest in you achieving your desire outcomes. They are likely to be highly experienced, highly skilled as a coach and totally focused on you achieving your success. Most highly successful people at some point have used the services of a coach. I don't know of any Olympic athlete who has become world class without the support of a professional coach.

When you're working with a coach and you've agreed your actions, commitments and time scales, it's a great motivator to know you are going to be held accountable if you choose not to follow through on those actions. I have a policy with some of my coaching clients that if they don't fulfil their commitments in between our sessions then they pay double for the next session! Nothing like a little bit of pain avoidance to keep someone motivated.

Surround yourself with positive, successful people and avoid spending time with people who don't believe in you, don't support you and are threatened by any success you create. In fact don't just avoid them – *run away* from them. Dream stealers can be very crafty and absolutely nobody has the right to take your dreams away from you!

Become a powerful peer yourself

Finally, one of the best ways to find your powerful peers is to become one yourself. Volunteer your services to those who you know you can help, step up and be a leader in your existing peer group and be generous to others as you create even more of your own success. The satisfaction and rewards you will enjoy will be immense.

Does it really work?

So, as you complete your journey to the New You, a more empowered, more focused, more confident version of your previous self, you may be wondering if it really is that simple and all you need to do is apply everything you've learnt here and your life will transform. Trust me on this: you have the ability to create any experience from your life that you desire. Yes, it may take time and, yes, it will take effort, but you absolutely can do it.

Let me finish by telling you a story about a client of mine. About 8 years ago this person was deeply, deeply unhappy, their marriage had ended unexpectedly, they were not achieving the required standards at work and were feeling the pressure, their finances were a mess (at the worst point they were 10 days away from declaring personal bankruptcy), their health was suffering and although family and friends were initially supportive, people became bored of the same old sob story and 'victim' mentality and started to drift away. They felt all alone, out of control, worthless and possessed very little self-confidence.

However, this person decided they wanted things to be different. Initially they didn't know exactly how it would all work out, but they made a commitment to making their life better. They consistently applied everything that you have learned in this book and as a result their life completely transformed. Their New You began to emerge, became stronger and better, until eventually, 8 years later, they are healthier, so much happier, have a fantastic relationship and family, their own successful business, have started a charity and it's difficult to even remember what the older version of themselves was like!

How do I know this? Because if you haven't guessed already, that was me! I'm not telling you this to impress you, simply to convince you that whatever your circumstances, whatever your desires, you have within you the power to create the newer, better version of yourself – the New You!

I wish *you* every success in *your* life.

SUMMARY

- Make it stick by building behaviours into your daily life.
- Continue to expose yourself to ongoing positive stimuli.
- Create a supportive environment that 'triggers' your positive behaviours.
- Surround yourself with powerful peers who believe in you, support you and hold you accountable.
- Enjoy the journey to discovering the New You!

Acknowledgements

This book could not have happened without the help of a uniquely gifted team of people who offer continued support in my life as well as to this project. Even if you are not mentioned here, please know that your efforts do not go unappreciated.

To Rachael Stock and all the team at Pearson for their amazing vision, guidance, and particularly to Rachael for her superb editing skills. You really are a genius at what you do!

To Helen Patten, without whom my life both personally and professionally would be in utter chaos: thank you for keeping the wolves at bay, giving me the time and space to focus on this project. Thank you to Phil Wiggins for your unwavering enthusiasm and commitment. You are both true ambassadors of our ethos and brand and I am privileged to have you in the team.

To my parents Pauline and Derek Cooper who have offered so much support to the decisions I make. To all the extended members of my family, even those I don't see as often as I would choose, and particularly to my sister-in-law and her husband, Claire and Kevin Love: you are both magical, maybe a tad bonkers but magical nonetheless, and a huge thank you for your practical support in helping me complete the work schedule necessary for this project.

To Christine and Michael Heppell, for being brilliant friends, and especially to Michael for your help and guidance in the practicalities of writing this book. To David Harper for your belief in me, particularly in the early days and for being my first fee-paying client, just when I needed it! To Dr Fiona Ellis, Zoe Laidler, Julie Whittaker and all the team at The Wellness Centre, who through your talents and skills enable me to work the gruelling schedule I put myself through, as well as taking care of the health of my family. To all the staff at Stepping Stones Nursery and to my childminder Jean Thackeray for taking such good care of my son. I am only able to do what I do when I know that Ty is well cared for, safe and happy. You are all such a special breed of people and I'm so grateful to you for providing such a high standard of care to my son.

To Dave Cook for many fond memories and some crucial defining moments in my life which have led me to this point thus far. To my dear friends Kathryn and Angela Armstrong, Tiffany Hodkinson and Karyn Parkinson, who have lived the highs, lows and lessons of my life so far, thank you for all your patience in listening to me ramble on. To my extra special friend Kate Spencer, thank you for being so 'PLU' as well as an awesome 'Ideas Man' and for always being at the end of the phone whenever I need some advice, support or guidance. To Amanda Morpeth for your enlightening spiritual friendship and for offering such beautiful reflections. To Colin Kendall for your very special friendship – your superb humour adds a freshness and lightness to my life.

To Neal Rose (aka Barry Scott) for being the best 'buddy' a girl could ever wish for, you are a brilliant person to pitch and catch against. I can never tell you any porky pies as you know me far too well and you always hold me to a higher standard! To all my friends within the Trainer and Crew community of The Anthony Robbins organization who continue to stretch my thinking, my vision and my self-belief; in particular Saskia Van Beers, Suzanne Burns, Mehul Bakrania, Steve Linder, Susie Mitchell, Connie Shotkey, Brigitte Sumner and David Taylor. You all add accountability and pace to my decisions – and just when I think I'm there, you stretch my thinking to a new higher level every time.

And finally, to my incredible husband Kevin Thomas, without

whom I absolutely would not be the person I am. You are the stable roots to my mad, dizzy, busy, blossom tree and I would not achieve the success I do without you and your unending support. So, for all the times I never made it home for dinner, for all the times I am too exhausted at the end of the day to even hold a conversation, for all the times I've needed you to drop everything and change plans in a heartbeat and for all the times I've put the needs of my vision first, you have never held a grudge, uttered a complaint or even grumbled under your breath – thank you doesn't even begin to describe how grateful I am for your unending unconditional love and support. This book would absolutely not have happened without you holding my hand every step of the way.

Seminars, Key Note Presentations, Media Appearances, Consultancy, Coaching, Books & Audio Programmes

Do you need to inject some fire and passion into your team? Do you need an inspirational female speaker at your next business event? Are you seeking a topical opinion for your panel or magazine? Or would you like to find out how to come along to a seminar or join a vibrant online community? Then act now and contact the team at Nicola's holding company, The Aurora Group, to find out more about the variety of services that Nicola and her team can offer.

Visit www.auroratraining.com
www.nicolacook.com

Email: info@auroratraining.com

Telephone 0870 766 9872
Fax 0870 766 9873

International +44 1207 582663

To be added to the free 'Northern Lights' online newsletter offering inspirational content and practical tips, simply email the word 'newsletter' to info@auroratraining.com

Visit Nicola's individual companies online:

- Aurora Training at www.auroratraining.com for seminars, corporate training, consultancy and coaching.
- Nicola Cook at www.nicolacook.com for media appearances, key note presentations and publication contributions.
- Aurora Foundation at www.aurorafoundation.co.uk for fundraising and work in the community.

For suggested further reading visit www.auroratraining.com